IDAHO

Inside and Out

R.G. ROBERTSON

photography by Karen A. Robertson

To the People of Idaho–

Past and Present

Idaho: Inside and Out
ISBN# 978-087004-6377

Idaho Echoes in Time was published by Tamarack Books Inc. in April 1998. *Idaho Inside and Out* contains all the stories in the original edition plus additional material that was written after the first edition's publication.

First Edition

Library of Congress Control Number: 2021939676

Cover and book design by Jocelyn Robertson

Printed in the United States of America
CAXTON PRESS
Caldwell, Idaho

TABLE OF CONTENTS

IDAHO

Inside and Out

INTRODUCTION

I'm a trivia junkie. Unusual facts, bizarre statistics, minutiae, the really weird stuff—I find all of it fascinating. Consequently for me, Idaho is heaven.

When my wife, Karen, and I moved to Idaho the first time, I knew little about the state beyond Sun Valley's ski runs. But as I began to read about Idaho and explore Idaho's historical sites and unique natural landmarks—places such as the City of Rocks, Craters of the Moon, Thousand Springs, Lemhi Pass, Borah Peak, Teton Basin—I quickly realized the Gem State was a trivia-lover's paradise.

Upon learning there was enough water in the Snake River Plain Aquifer to cover the entire state to a depth of four feet and that 20,000 years ago a wall of water over 2,000 feet high scoured Idaho's panhandle, my mind went into overdrive with comparisons. For example, empty the aquifer into the Mediterranean Sea and it will rise 3½ inches. And 2,000 feet of water—that's as though someone stacked up two Chrysler Buildings. You remember, the New York skyscraper that King Kong climbed while clutching Fay Wray in the 1933 movie. The possibilities for illustration are endless.

As did most of my generation, I grew up on television and comic-book tales of Wyatt Earp and Bat Masterson. When I first came across the unlikely name Orlando "Rube" Robbins, little did I suspect it belonged to an Idaho lawman whose exploits as a pistoleer equaled in every way those of his more famous contemporaries.

Another of my tidbits resulted from a trip from Sun Valley to Boise during the springtime. After driving past acres of blue camas west of Fairfield, I sought to find out more about this lovely flower that each May and June carpets so many of the state's marshes. During my research I was surprised to discover this innocent lily had ignited a bloody Indian war.

As I related the things I was learning about Idaho to my long-suffering friends—including some who had lived here all their lives—I saw a void. Many who would normally roll their eyes at the mention of history or geology said "I didn't know that," as they listened to how the Astorians abandoned their canoes at the falls of Caldron Linn. Afterwards, a few of my friends pressed me for directions so they could visit the Snake River's most southern point, where the volcanic walls squeeze the boiling current into a 40-foot-wide gap.

Thinking that other Idahoans and Idaho visitors may have an interest in the state's past, I began writing a newspaper column called "Idaho Inside Out." During the mid-1990s my stories appeared regularly in a number of Idaho newspapers. Then in 1998 Tamarack Books published a collection of my articles, titled *Idaho Echoes in Time*.

Karen Robertson, who is a freelance photographer, and I visited all the locales where my stories are set. Our journeys took us from Porthill to Franklin and from Weiser to Driggs as we criss-crossed the state multiple times.

My goal has always been to make the past come alive. I hope my stories awaken an interest in you the reader, prompting you to hike up the Menan Buttes in order to gaze at the confluence of Henry's Fork and the main Snake River or to stroll along a remnant of the Mullan Road. I never intended *Idaho Echoes in Time* to be an encompassing history or geology textbook. Instead, it is a series of stories about the myriad people and geologic events that collectively contribute to what is Idaho.

Idaho Echoes in Time has been out of print for a number of years. When my wife and I recently moved back to Idaho after a decade and a half absence, I decided to revise and republish *Idaho Echoes* under the title *Idaho Inside and Out*. In addition to the stories that were in the original book, this new edition includes stories that were written after *Idaho Echoes in Time* went to press.

Like *Idaho Echoes in Time*, *Idaho Inside and Out* is divided in two sections. "Part One: A Land Formed by Fire and Flood" is a series of essays, or as I prefer to think of them, snapshots that trace the corporeal formation of Idaho. If read in sequence, these chapters will recount the state's geologic life, from its separation from the supercontinent Pangaea 250 million years ago, to its adolescence as it grew in area and height, its middle age when it was sculpted by lava, and its mature years when rivers of water and ice carved deep canyons in its earthly flesh.

"Idaho's Swath of Fire" is perhaps the most controversial chapter in this section. Although most geologists agree the Snake River Plain was formed when the North American Plate slid over a permanent hot spot in the earth's mantle, not all of them think the hot spot was created 17 million years ago by a large meteorite that blasted an immense hole in southeastern Oregon. That this theory will eventually be proved correct remains to be seen.

The scope of *Idaho Inside and Out* has dictated I omit certain pieces in Idaho's geologic puzzle. But in my defense, let me repeat it was never my intention to write a classical text. Instead, I want my stories to paint a mosaic that will awaken an interest to further study in the non-geologist reader.

"Part Two: A People Forged by Courage" looks at Idaho's transients and kinsmen through snippets of time, beginning with Lewis and Clark and continuing until Jim Curran and the construction of the Sun Valley Resort. Rather than write about the pillars of government and industry, I've chosen among Idaho's many visitors, immigrants, and Native Americans, seeking those who have done something memorable, whether good or bad. A few, such as Ira Perrine, left a lasting mark, whereas others, like Al Faussett, had no more influence than a wisp of smoke. Yet no matter how big or small their roles, without their contributions, Idaho wouldn't be what it is today.

The stories in Part Two are presented chronologically, but unlike those in Part One, it's unnecessary to read them in sequence in order to grasp some larger understanding of Idaho's history. I've gathered my material from numerous sources, many of which offer differing reports of the same events. For example, while researching Peg Leg Annie, I read a clipping which said she had only one foot amputated and another which said two. I've also read at least two versions about where her rescuers found her after the blizzard that frostbit her feet ended. In deciding what is correct in this tale and in others, I've employed corroborating articles, logic, and occasionally, an educated guess. I ask you to consider this when one of my stories disagrees with an account you have seen elsewhere.

In a similar vein, historical events may be given different interpretations. For the most part, the opening of the American west was written from the perspective of white civilization instead of from that of the Native Americans. Revisionist historians try to redress this imbalance by blaming Anglo society for every ill that has befallen the Indians since the arrival of Christopher Columbus. Certainly the "dead white males" who settled (or stole, depending on your view) Idaho did much to harm Indian culture, but the modern reader would do well to examine past actions in light of the mores of the times and not the political correctness of today.

Idaho Inside and Out will no more settle this dispute than did its predecessor. That isn't the goal of either edition. The book seeks neither to be an apologist for white transgression nor to ignore the plight of the native tribes that were crushed by the influx of soldiers, miners, farmers, and shopkeepers. I've attempted to write my stories objectively, giving the views and motivations of all parties on an issue, then letting you, the reader, determine right from wrong. I trust I've succeeded.

Finally, I've included an addendum to the chapters—"Sights to See"—giving directions to the pertinent sites so you can visit them. I've also described activities and scenic points that will make the visits more meaningful as well as fun. I urge you to see as much of Idaho as possible. Gazing on the Snake River Plain from atop Big Southern Butte and peering down at Hells Canyon from Sheep Rock in the Seven Devils Mountains are experiences I'll always cherish. If this book gets you to stand on the cliff above Caldron Linn or to pull off the highway and read a state historical sign, it will have accomplished its purpose.

Part One

A LAND FORMED BY FIRE AND FLOOD

McCALL
Idaho's Surf City

Imagine driving to the western limits of McCall and looking not at green forests but at crashing, saltwater waves and endless miles of Pacific beach. Geologists tell us such a scene is exactly what we would have seen had we been alive 250 million years ago.

At that time central Idaho formed the western edge of Pangaea, a supercontinent that included most of North and South America, Europe, Africa, and Asia. Beyond Idaho's shoreline was a vast ocean. Although the ocean held islands and the remnants of other continents that had long since split apart, no large landmass lay between Idaho and the Asian coastline. Eastward from McCall was nothing but land, an expanse that extended all the way to China and Siberia.

Then a rift formed in the earth's mantle, and the North and South American plates broke loose from Pangaea and slowly moved west, in a way much like two rowboats tethered bow to stern slipping their moorings and drifting away from a large wooden pier. The North and South American plates floated on a belt of molten rock deep within the earth. As the distance between the two plates and the rest of Pangaea widened, water flowed into the void, creating the Atlantic Ocean. The Atlantic grew at 1½ inches per year, a process that continues today.

At the Mid-Atlantic Ridge where the split occurred, the sea floor widened as lava oozed from the earth's mantle and formed new oceanic crust. Simultaneously, over near McCall and all along Idaho's western border, the Pacific crust began sinking into a trench beneath the advancing but more buoyant North American plate. The same thing also happened off the coast of western South America.

Hells Canyon and the Snake River as seen from the Kinney Point turnoff in the Seven Devils Mountains.

Each year the breadth of the Pacific Ocean was reduced by 1½ inches as Idaho collected the islands and continental debris that littered the shrinking Pacific. Being too light to sink, these bits of land slammed against the west coast and stuck. The Seven Devils Mountains of the Hells Canyon Wilderness are volcanic Pacific islands that were welded to Idaho 100 million years ago. Each succeeding collision inched Idaho farther and farther inland.

Meanwhile, these collisions and the subduction of the Pacific crust fractured, wrinkled, and folded the North American plate as if it were a small rug on a polished hardwood floor being shoved against a wall. All of this action gave birth to the Rocky Mountains.

The heat caused by the Pacific crust diving into the earth's mantle melted the North American plate's basement rocks, forcing up granite magma into the wrinkled welts beneath Idaho, thereby causing the state's burgeoning mountains to grow taller. But unfortunately for coming generations of Idaho mountaineers, internal pressures forced a number of these unstable chunks—some in the Frank Church-River of No Return Wilderness were nearly a dozen miles thick—to slide east into Montana. As the masses of granite moved, they piled the land before them into more mountains.

Having lost all that weight, Idaho popped up like an empty river barge that suddenly loses its cargo. However, the state's new peaks are only half as tall as the ones that were shed.

Today, the North American plate continues its 1½-inch annual drift toward Hawaii. In time, Oahu and Maui will fuse with California, Oregon, and Washington, and Idahoan surfers will have farther to drive before they can catch a wave.

SIGHTS TO SEE

Seven Devils Mountains

From US 95 in Council, take the Hornet Creek Road (later called the Council-Cuprum Road) 29 miles west to Bear Junction and turn left toward Cuprum. In 7.2 miles swing right at the T and drive one mile to Cuprum. Continue another 10.4 miles to the Kinney Point turnoff.

The single-lane track to the point (½ mile) is rough but possible for cars.

Sheep Rock (a National Natural Landmark)

Located 2.2 miles beyond the Kinney Point turnoff. Hells Canyon and the Seven Devils can be seen from both locations.

IDAHO'S
Swath of Fire

Stretching across southern Idaho like the upper torso of a medieval dragon, the Snake River Plain's fiery snout now reaches into Yellowstone National Park. A cursory glance at the state's topography illustrates that this sweep of land is unique.

If not for the Snake River Plain, Idaho's mountains would extend uninterrupted from Porthill into Nevada and Utah. Yet in a broad swath from the Owyhee River past Jerome and Rexburg and on toward the Continental Divide, the country lies flat, as if bladed by a gargantuan bulldozer.

Some geologists think a massive meteorite landed in southeastern Oregon about 17 million years ago. The force of its impact rent the earth's crust, punching a hole in the mantle. That hole—more properly called a hot spot—released an avalanche of basalt lava, which flooded into eastern Washington and the lowlands of western Idaho, creating the Columbia Plateau.

Near the same time, immense faults began splitting the Rocky Mountains of western Idaho and north-central Nevada. As these rifts pulled apart the earth's crust, long, generally north-south running sections of bedrock started to rise and fall, forming the valleys and mountains called Basin and Range.

Meanwhile, the North American plate continued drifting west, as it had been doing for well over 200 million years. Being in the mantle, the hot spot didn't move. Instead, much like an acetylene torch held stationary beneath a sliding sheet of steel, the hot spot seared a path across southern Idaho at 1½ inches per year. Today the hot spot smolders beneath the northwestern corner of Wyoming, thrilling tourists in Yellowstone National Park with steaming vents, hot gurgling mud pots, and erupting geysers.

Bruneau Canyon Overlook.

Scientists have traced the hot spot by the resurgent calderas—collapsed volcanoes—it has left in its wake. From Grasmere to Magic Reservoir to Mud Lake to upper Henry's Fork, the age of each succeeding caldera grows progressively younger.

The Island Park Caldera in Fremont County has a diameter of nearly 20 miles. The ash discharged by its first eruption 2.1 million years ago covered the countryside with rhyolite—so much, in fact, that Mount St. Helens would need to explode 600 times in order to match its output. The ash was so hot it congealed into a thick layer of pinkish-gray stone. The modern world has never experienced such energy and resulting devastation. No atomic or hydrogen bomb blast has ever equaled the power released by the Island Park Caldera.

So far the hot spot sitting beneath Yellowstone National Park has ignited three explosions. The most recent one occurred 600,000 years ago. Few geologists think it will be the last. With a 600,000-year interval separating each of these three eruptions, another is certainly due.

Just as the hot spot appears to have moved east—because the North American plate where Idaho resides is moving west over the stationary hot spot—so, too, does the Basin and Range faulting. The shield volcanoes that coated the Snake River Plain with its basalt veneer are a recent consequence of this faulting. Presently, the leading edge of the Basin and Range has entered Utah's Wasatch Mountains, a point directly south of the Yellowstone Caldera.

As for the future of the Snake River Plain, it will continue to grow. So long as the North American plate drifts across the Pacific Ocean, the hot spot will kindle its way toward Billings, Montana.

Upper Mesa Falls.

Bruneau Canyon Overlook

From Mountain Home, follow Idaho State Road 51 south 20 miles to Bruneau. Turn left on Hot Springs Road. In 7.8 miles where the pavement ends, keep left on Clover Creek Road. In another 8.1 miles turn right at the sign for the Bruneau Canyon Overlook, 3.2 miles beyond.

Allegedly named for Baptiste Bruneau, who trapped here in the early 1800s, the Bruneau River has cut an 800-foot gorge through the basalt and rhyolite of the Bruneau-Jarbridge Caldera. Hikes along the canyon rim, up- and downstream from the overlook, offer stunning views of the river as well as the high desert. During the late spring and early summer, watch for kayakers braving the Bruneau's white water. **Also, beware of rattlesnakes.**

Author standing at Big Springs, the source of the Henry's Fork River.

Lower Mesa Falls.

Island Park Caldera

About 10 miles north of Ashton US 20 climbs Big Bend Ridge, a U-shaped rim of rhyolite which bounds the Island Park Caldera. Totaling approximately 350 square miles, this dead volcano is the world's largest "recognized" caldera. The highway cuts the crater's northern boundary near Island Park.

While driving across the caldera, observe its western escarpment, which rises 1,200 feet above the Snake River Plain. The caldera's eastern lip lies beneath more recent lava flows from Yellowstone National Park. During the Island Park Caldera's initial eruption 2.1 million years ago, it rained hot ash over an area the size of New Jersey. Following the volcano's smaller, final explosion 800,000 years later, its magma chamber collapsed, forming the immense basin that is visible today.

Spring snow on Big Southern Butte.

YOU CAN SEE FOREVER

Viewed from atop Big Southern Butte near Arco, the upper Snake River Plain appears to roll and heave as though it were some sort of primeval, petrified ocean. On a clear day you can see the Teton Mountains painting a steel-gray backdrop for the eastern horizon. To the north the White Knob, Lost River, Lemhi, and Beaverhead ranges resemble giant ribs arching out from Idaho's flat, lava-rippled belly.

If you look west from Idaho Falls, Big Southern and its lessor neighbors, Middle and East Buttes, interrupt the landscape much the way volcanic islands such as Hawaii and Maui protrude from the uniformity of the sea. As you gaze over the plain, these mounds of rhyolite seize your eye as if they were magnets.

During the early 19th century, the buttes guided fur trappers such as Jedediah Smith and Alexander Ross. A few years later, Oregon-bound emigrants stared at them for hour after endless hour as their exhausted oxen trudged over the region's hoof-splitting rocks.

Today US 26 parallels Goodale's Cutoff of the Oregon Trail as it knifes between Big Southern and the smaller twins. From inside an air conditioned car speeding past Atomic City, Middle and East Buttes appear impressive. But from the 7,560-foot summit of Big Southern Butte, they look as imposing as two dwarf pines alongside a Sequoia redwood.

Although geologically modern, the buttes trace their ancestry back five or six million years, when violent rhyolitic volcanism erupted across the eastern Snake River Plain. As the North American plate drifted westward, the hot spot that produced these eruptions gradually moved under Yellowstone National Park. Taking their place was a milder form of volcanism that began when the earth's upper mantle started to melt 31 to 37 miles below the surface. Like spilled molasses on a warm day, basalt lava oozed from fissures in the underlying rock until it covered the rhyolite with a black crust.

Then 600,000 years ago in an anticlimactic conclusion to the caldera era of the Snake River Plain, a dome of rhyolite, much like an expanding pressure ridge on an asphalt highway, elbowed its way through the basalt and formed East Butte. Middle Butte followed, but with less force. Its rhyolitic summit lies buried under a mountain of basalt.

In a final hurrah around 300,000 years ago, Big Southern Butte thrust its bulk into the daylight. It climbed slowly without the explosive fanfare of early rhyolitic eruptions, as if it were an exhausted Atlas struggling to shrug his massive shoulders beneath the weight of the world. When the forces driving Big Southern Butte stopped, the dome loomed 2,500 feet above the plain. Rivers of molten basalt have continued to flood across Big Southern Butte's domain, with some lapping at its base. The last one welled out of Idaho's Great Rift about the time Julius Caesar was born.

Now a National Natural Landmark, Big Southern Butte provides unimpeded views for nearly 100 miles. No matter if you drive the jeep road to the top or hike up one of the butte's crumbly flanks (both of which this author and his wife have done), the panorama is worth the effort.

Big Southern Butte

From I-15 Exit 93 near Blackfoot drive northwest 29 miles on US 26, turning west at the sign for Atomic City. For those coming from Arco, the turnoff is 6.8 miles southeast of the US 20/26 junction. Follow the paved spur road 1.4 miles to a T at the edge of town. Turn left (south) for 1.3 miles, and then go right on a gravel road. After 3.9 miles cross the Union Pacific railroad tracks. From here on, the road varies between dirt and cinder. In one mile bear left and drive another 8.7 miles around the Butt's south and west sides. At the signed intersection, swing right toward Big Butte Lookout. In 3.6 miles you'll come to a ranch and Frenchman's Cabin. Turn right and drive up the Big Butte Lookout jeep road. It is 4.6 *extremely rough* miles to the summit. Should you choose to hike cross-country up one of the Butte's flanks, be aware the rock is loose. (The author and his wife have summited the butte by doing both.)

The road to the top of Big Southern Butte is recommended for ***high clearance, 4-wheel-drive vehicles only****. Idaho's desert roads can be treacherous when wet. Always carry a backcountry map and emergency supplies including water.*

GROWING A MOUNTAIN

At 8:06 Friday morning, October 28, 1983, Hilda Goddard was slicing vegetables in her kitchen a few miles from the Mackay Reservoir when she heard a noise that sounded like a low-flying jet fighter. At the same time a dozen miles farther north, Wiley Smith was enjoying a last sip of coffee before heading out to work. In the next instant their worlds began to shake.

In the Goddard home, cans and jars jumped off their shelves. Hilda's elderly mother lay in bed, too disoriented to stand. Outside, Hilda's husband and sons watched the semi-trailer they were preparing to load buck and heave with the energy of a rodeo bull.

Measuring 7.3 on the Richter Scale, the Borah Peak Earthquake lasted about seven seconds. In Thousand Springs Valley just below Idaho's tallest mountain, the ground under the Smith ranch sank nine feet, while Mt. Borah grew 12 inches. Two miles from Wiley's breakfast table, the land ripped, forming an escarpment 21 miles long and in many places six feet high.

In Challis, two children were crushed by a falling building. Shock waves raced through the earth's crust, rattling windows 500 miles from the epicenter. For a couple of hours after the quake, water spouted from Chilly Butte, and the Mackay Reservoir bubbled as if it were a caldron. On the valley floor, sand boils created dwarf craters, and 400 billion gallons of water poured forth from new springs. A year later, Parsons Creek on the Goddard property was still flowing two feet above normal.

In southern Idaho, seismic events such as the Borah Peak Earthquake have been going on for 17 million years. Known by geologists as Basin and Range faulting, these tremors have inched

Borah Peak Earthquake Escarpment knifing along the base of the Big Lost River Mountains.

from west to east across the state, erecting mountain chains such as the White Knobs and Lost Rivers.

Idaho sits in the northern part of the Basin and Range Province, which had its genesis in southeastern Oregon and now extends into Mexico and eastern Idaho. The entire province includes over 150 mountain ranges and their defining valleys. They run generally north-south.

North America's Basin and Range structure is caused by forces within the earth's mantle that are slowly stretching and thinning the crust. The distance between the Atlantic and Pacific seaboards is increasing at one-half inch per year as the North American plate drifts toward Hawaii at an annual rate three times that amount. Valleys such as Thousand Springs are growing wider, whereas the mountains towering above them are pushing toward the clouds.

This mountain-building occurs because the upper rocks in the North American plate's western crust are being split into gigantic blocks. These brittle, sub-surface blocks—some a dozen or more miles thick—ride on slippery, putty-like rocks that float on the earth's mantle. The breaks between the blocks are known as faults, and it's along these that the blocks slide.

The earth's 2,000-mile-thick mantle behaves like a liquid, although it is solid. The mantle's extremely high temperature keeps it viscous, and pressure from the buoyant crust prevents it from melting. Heat causes the rocks closest to the mantle to take on its malleable properties.

As an analogy, imagine placing a large granite block on a thick sheet of India rubber. Now set the weighted rubber in a vat of warm molasses. Next saw the granite into domino-size pieces, cutting each of them at an angle of 60 degrees. If you and a friend pull the opposite sides of the sheet, the stretching rubber will increase the spaces between the granite pieces, causing them to fall against one another. Peer closely and you'll see that the pieces' higher, leading edges form miniature mountain ridges, whereas the low points separating the ridges resemble tiny valleys.

On a much bigger scale, as the rocks beneath southern Idaho are broken into blocks by the stretching crust, they tilt against one another, forming mountain ranges and basins. Gravity, rain, and streams erode the peaks, bringing down detritus and filling the valley floors with sediment. This added weight further unbalances the blocks, sinking the valleys more while lifting the mountains.

A similar thing happens when a swimmer crawls onto an air mattress floating in a swimming pool. The portion of the mattress supporting the swimmer sags beneath his or her weight as the unweighted part of the mattress rises.

In the real world, of course, the erosion occurs over tens of thousands of years. Its deposits slowly build up pressure on the unstable blocks, which is periodically released in a few heart-stopping seconds.

Just as Basin and Range faulting has widened the distance from Boise to Idaho Falls, it's now working to pull Victor away from Pocatello. In the future, eastern Idaho will continue to experience earthquakes such as the one that shook the Goddard and Smith households during the autumn of 1983.

SIGHTS TO SEE

Borah Peak Earthquake Escarpment Interpretive Site

From Arco drive north on US 93. The highway follows the Big Lost River Valley, which was formed by the same Basin and Range faulting that built the Lost River and White Knob mountains on either side. Approximately 22 miles north of Mackay turn right (northeast) on Doublesprings Pass Road; the interpretive site is 2½ miles beyond.

The clearly-visible scarp runs along the base of the Lost River Range. Continue driving up the Doublesprings Pass Road for stunning views of Borah Peak.

FIRE ABOVE,
Water Below

The lava fields of Idaho's eastern Snake River Plain cover an area slightly larger than Maryland. They are a visual testament to the volcanic forces that shaped our state.

For eons magma rose from the depths of the mantle and then spurted and oozed as lava from the nearly 1,000 inconspicuous shield volcanoes that dot the plain's tortured contours. As recently as 2,100 years ago titanium-rich Blue Dragon lava spewed from the fissures of Craters of the Moon National Monument. Today, a bed of basalt underlies the plain's patchwork farms that are lush with potato plants and hay.

When driving past the Snake River Plain's blackened buttes, cinder cones, and collapsed lava tubes, it is easy to imagine a time when Idaho ran orange with fire and molten rock.

Bouncing along the Carey-Kimama Road in early autumn gives a sense of how uncompromising this country really is. Although the lava no longer flows, its imprint is everywhere. Away from the hardened basalt, the sun works in harmony with the desert sand, begrudging the sagebrush and wheatgrass the scantiest drop of moisture.

In this arid landscape who would think that below the surface lies enough water to cover all Idaho to a depth of four feet. Layers of porous basalt, some over a mile thick, soak up water like a thirsty sponge. Waterways such as the Big Lost River carry snowmelt from the neighboring peaks to the upper Snake River Plain. Near Howe that stream seeps into the Snake River Plain Aquifer. Percolating through the pervious rock, the water traverses nearly 100 miles before gushing to daylight at Thousand Springs. Trickling through the aquifer at the rate of two to 10 feet per day, water we now see issuing from Niagara Springs fell as snow in the Pioneer Mountains when Thomas Jefferson was being bounced on his father's knee.

It would take 59 American Falls Reservoirs to equal the amount of water in the top 100 feet of the aquifer. If completely drained, its water could fill Lake Erie. Although the aquifer's upper reaches are the most permeable, in places the aquifer is estimated to be 5,500 feet deep.

Since Julion "Duke" Clawson first drilled into the aquifer just north of Rupert in 1947, its waters have greened vast acres of desert loess. Several thousand wells now tap its liquid treasure, providing sustenance to over 130,000 Idahoans.

Before irrigated farming became widespread, the aquifer obtained its water from streams such as the Big Lost River and from the eight to 14 inches of annual precipitation that soak into the plain. As more and more rangeland has been cultivated, water from irrigation has become the aquifer's central replenishing source.

In the mid-1950s the aquifer was at its fullest, but in the years since then, farmers have learned to irrigate more efficiently. The wide use of sprinklers means less water is available to seep into the ground. In some places the aquifer is 15 percent lower than it was just 40 years ago. However, it still holds more water than it did in 1900.

Aa lava sculptures at Craters of the Moon National Monument.

Niagara Springs: The largest of Idaho's Thousand Springs.

SIGHTS TO SEE

Craters of the Moon National Monument

Located on US 20/26/93, 19 miles west of Arco. Except for certain holidays, the visitor center is open year-round.

Niagara Springs (the largest of the Snake River's Thousand Springs)

From I-84 Exit 157 near Wendell, drive south 7.8 miles on Orchard Valley Road. The springs are located 0.1 mile past the Niagara Springs Steelhead Fish Hatchery.

IDAHO'S
Thousand Springs

On September 2, 1852, Parthenia Blank noted in her diary the sight of two massive springs bursting from the dark cliffs overlooking the Snake River. The springs were about a mile apart, and their discharges plunged 100 feet down the steep rock faces before flowing into the Snake.

During America's great westward migration, Parthenia and other diarists recorded seeing innumerable springs on the right side of the Snake River where its channel doglegs toward Upper Salmon Falls. By most estimates, 1,000 separate springs gushed from the bluffs that tower above this stretch of river. The springs were so profuse that a few Oregon-bound travelers wrote that the canyon walls wept.

The water that feeds Idaho's Thousand Springs comes from the Snake River Plain Aquifer. The aquifer had its genesis about two million years ago when giant vents, such as the Great Rift, and hundreds of shield volcanoes began flooding southern Idaho with surge after surge of basalt lava. The viscous basalt spread over the landscape like thick hot syrup. When it encountered water, the basalt congealed into rounded rocks, known as pillows.

Between eruptions, sediment and rubble collected on the most recent flow, only to be covered a bit later by yet another blanket of basalt. Over the ages, layer piled atop layer until the eastern Snake River Plain resembled an immense lava sandwich, in some places over 5,000 feet thick.

The Snake River Plain Aquifer behaves like a giant sponge. Rain and snowmelt from a drainage the size of Indiana is carried by rivers and streams to the Snake River Plain, where the runoff seeps into the multilayered bed of lava, basalt pillows, and rubble. Drawn by gravity at the rate of two to 10 feet per day, this under-

Twisted tree and wildflowers amid the lava at Craters of the Moon National Monument.

ground water percolates through the permeable layers of rubble and pillows as it steadily makes its way south and west toward the Snake River.

Much of the water travels over 100 miles before being discharged into the Snake near American Falls and at the Thousand Springs region southeast of Hagerman. Each year the aquifer replenishes the Snake with enough water to fill nearly one-third of Utah's Lake Powell. That's nearly two million gallons for every man, woman, and child living in Idaho.

The Hagerman Valley contains 17 percent of America's biggest cold water springs. During the summer when nearly the entire Snake River is drained into irrigation canals above Milner Dam, the springs between Twin Falls and Hagerman supply virtually all the river's flow until the Snake merges with the Bruneau River a few miles east of Grand View.

Today the Thousand Springs look far different than they did a century and a half ago when Parthenia Blank described two of them in her diary. Much of their flow has been harnessed to turn the turbines of Idaho Power. The springs have also been diverted for fish hatcheries, since their constant 58-degree water is perfect for raising trout and steelhead. Every year nearly 25,000 tons of trout are harvested from the numerous fish farms that dot the banks of the Snake River upstream from Bliss.

The Hagerman National Fish Hatchery, which was built in 1933, runs 36 million gallons of crystal-clear spring water through its rearing tanks and raceways every day. Each April the hatchery ships over 1.5 million young steelheads to the Sawtooth Valley where they're released into the Salmon River and its tributaries.

During the following two to three months, these smolts fight their way downstream to the Snake River and then the Columbia. Those that are lucky enough to survive predators, dams, pollutants, warm water reservoirs, and a myriad of other deadly hazards eventually grow to adulthood in the Pacific Ocean.

Although modern man has altered many of the Thousand Springs to where Parthenia Blank would no longer recognize them, the ones that remain unchanged are among Idaho's most splendid sights.

SIGHTS TO SEE

Thousand Springs Scenic Byway

From downtown Buhl drive west about 15 miles on US 30. Look to the right across the Snake River to see the springs cascading down from the cliffs.

Hagerman National Fish Hatchery

Continue on US 30 two miles past the Thousand Springs viewpoints to the Snake River Bridge; 1.6 miles beyond the bridge turn right at the hatchery sign on County Road 2925S. In 0.5 mile turn right on 1050E; at the Y one mile later, keep right on National Fish Hatchery Road. The hatchery is 0.6 mile ahead.

The Hagerman National Fish Hatchery is open to the public year-round. The outdoor raceways contain steelhead fry. After "smoltification" each spring, these fish are released into the wild. Between the end of March and mid-May, over 40 tanker-loads of steelhead smolts are trucked to the Salmon River drainage. Three-quarters of these fish are released at the Sawtooth Fish Hatchery south of Stanley, where their instincts will eventually guide them back to spawn. When the adult steelheads return from the Pacific Ocean, hatchery personnel collect their eggs and sperm and induce fertilization.

Behind the Administration Building, Hatchery #1 contains tanks of rainbow trout fingerlings. Each May the hatchery releases over 100,000 six-inch rainbows, followed in September by a smaller release of ten-inch trout.

Fifty yards to the right of the Administration Building are picnic tables and a display pool containing white sturgeon and adult rainbow trout. From the picnic grounds a nature trail leads toward the bluffs. Climb the metal stairway to a series of small aquifer-fed springs. The trail follows the contours of the cliff, offering stunning views of the hatchery and Snake River.

Minnie Miller Falls

This large spring is visible from US 30. To see it close-up, leave the Hagerman National Fish Hatchery, returning 0.6 mile to the start of National Fish Hatchery Road. At the intersection, turn hard right, heading uphill on 3000S. In 0.8 mile, the road swings right, becoming 1200E. Wind through farm land for another 2.7 miles, turning right on One Thousand Springs Grade. The Minnie Miller Preserve, a power station, picnic grounds, and path to the base of the falls are located at the bottom of the gravel road.

Minnie Miller Falls with the Snake River in the background.

FROM FIRE TO ICE

The Shoshone Indian Ice Caves

During the 1890s, summer visitors to Shoshone, Idaho, often wilted when stepping down from the passenger coaches of the Oregon Short Line Railroad. The temperature in August and early September frequently tipped 100 degrees. Imagine their pleasant surprise when these thirsty travelers ventured into one of the town's 22 saloons and were offered iced beer.

For countless ages before the white man ever set foot on the Snake River Plain, the Shoshone Indians and their prehistoric relatives knew about an ice cave just south of Black Butte (near the present-day Magic Reservoir, off Idaho State Road 75). Each year during their migration to the camas fields below the Soldier Mountains, the Indians tarried by the cave for a few days.

Legend says the Evil Spirit of Darkness lured *Edahow*, the Shoshone Princess of Light and Fertility, into the cave and imprisoned her in an icy tomb. Over the years the tribe awaited the time when the ice would melt, once more allowing *Edahow* to nurture the People of the Snake.

In 1884, 10-year-old Alfa Kinsey was herding his father's sheep across the lava-buckled plain beside Black Butte, when he "discovered" a cave filled with ice. Soon some resourceful businessmen from the nearby hamlet of Shoshone began harvesting the ice and freighting it by wagon to the town's saloons and restaurants. The enterprise folded in 1900 but not until it had excavated over 50,000 cubic feet of ice from the cave.

Ten years later, spelunkers slithered into a second chamber, where they encountered more ice. After reaching a third and final chamber, they found it plugged with an ice slab measuring 21 feet high by 38 feet wide.

With the front cave no longer being quarried, the ice grew until eventually threatening to choke it shut. In 1930 the entrance to the first cavern was enlarged to afford easier passage. This ill-considered "enhancement" allowed the warmer outside air to invade the caves. The ice slowly but steadily began to melt.

In 1936 the caves came under the auspices of the Federal Government's Works Progress Administration (WPA), which added amenities making the three caverns more accessible to the public. By the following year the large ice block in the last chamber had lost one-third of its volume.

That winter when the caves were left unattended, vandals skirted the receding ice wall and dynamited a hole in the rear chamber. Now having two entrances, the sweltering summer air funneled through the caves with a vengeance. Within five years the ice was only a memory.

The Shoshone Indian Ice Caves had their genesis during an eruption of Black Butte, one of the many shield volcanoes dotting the Snake River Plain. A river of basalt lava oozed from the crater, flowing like molasses on a frosty morning.

The molten stream meandered south, following the land's dips and gullies. As it sluggishly seared a path across the countryside, this tide of hot viscous rock cooled at its surface while its orange center remained in flux. A crust hardened around the fiery core that was continually fed by lava spewing from Black Butte. When the volcano eventually exhausted its reservoir of magma, the fluid rock emptied out of its basalt tunnel, leaving a hollow tube many miles long.

As the lava tube aged, parts of its roof collapsed, forming rubble-strewn sinkholes and sealing the remaining sections of the tube into caverns, some nearly 50 feet tall. A couple of miles south of Black Butte, two portions of the tube crumpled, enclosing three vaulted chambers. In time a bit of the ceiling collapsed in the eastern-most chamber, opening a small hole.

For countless winters, dense, cold air sank through this hole, displacing the warmer air. During Idaho's torrid summers, the hot outside air remained above the caves, unable to penetrate the heavier, frigid air within. Water seeping into the Shoshone Indian Ice Caves froze, in time nearly filling the three caverns with ice. The caves behaved like a "natural refrigerator" until modern man altered their configuration.

From 1941 until the mid-1950s, the damaged Shoshone Indian Ice Caves sat vacant. Then Russell Robinson took over their management and began to experiment, hoping to get the ice to re-form. He patched the rear hole blasted by vandals 20 years before and reduced the size of the front entrance. To his delight, the ice reappeared.

Today the 1,700-foot-long Shoshone Indian Ice Caves have an ice floor that varies from eight to 30 feet thick. An electric pump removes 50 gallons of water per day from the caves. If it didn't, four feet of new ice would accumulate each year, eventually filling the caves to their arched ceilings.

Black Butte: Lava source for the Shoshone Indian Ice Caves.

Shoshone Indian Ice Caves

Located on Idaho State Road 75, 17 miles north of Shoshone and 12 miles south of the US 20/ID 75 intersection.

Be sure to take a jacket or sweater for the tour, since the air inside the caves is cold, even in August.

Black Butte

The broken summit sits 1½ miles west of Idaho State Road 75 and is clearly visible from the highway. A faint, unmarked Jeep trail 1.2 miles north of the turnoff to the ice caves leads to the volcano's rim. **Only high clearance vehicles are advised.** (The author and his wife walked most of this route despite having a Jeep.)

The author entering the Shoshone Indian Ice Caves.

Contoured hayfield at the foot of North Menan Butte.

MENAN BUTTES

About 20 miles north of Idaho Falls, Henry's Fork and the Snake River converge. The Menan Buttes loom over this confluence as though they are petrified mounds of Rocky Road ice cream. A close inspection of these twin volcanoes reveals a composite of brown tuff intermixed with white quartzite pebbles, which puts you in mind of a chocolate sundae laden with miniature marshmallows.

Thirty thousand years ago Henry's Fork and the Snake merged a mile or so northwest of where they do now. For countless ages these rivers had deposited gravel, clay, sand, and silt at their junction, forming a thick alluvial fan that was saturated by snowmelt floods each spring. Hundreds of feet beneath this moist delta sat the Snake River Plain Aquifer, with its multiple layers of water-permeated basalt.

Across southeastern Idaho, internal forces in the mantle stretched the earth's crust, creating rifts. In the mountains north and south of the Snake River Plain, this Basin and Range faulting, as geologists call it, continued nudging the Lost River Mountains, the Portneufs, and their sister peaks toward the clouds as erosion sought to carry their outer layers to the valleys' floors.

On the Snake River Plain, lava oozed from splits such as the Great Rift and from the numerous shield volcanoes that dotted the landscape. Flowing slowly like a syrup spill on a cold January morning, each new eruption smothered the plain with yet another porous blanket of black basalt.

Below the delta formed by the Henry's Fork and Snake River confluence, the continental crust fractured, allowing magma to rise toward the surface. Pressured by heat from the earth's mantle, the liquid basalt welled from its reservoir, sluicing through the cracks as though they were a subterranean pipeline.

Striking first the aquifer and then the sodden floodplain

above, the red-hot magma flashed the water into a mighty steam explosion. Along a three-mile fissure, massive clouds of basalt cinders, river rock, and ash burst into the sky. As the heavier rubble rained back to earth, it started building two rings of tuff around the spewing craters.

Wave after wave of magma surged upwards, vaporizing the groundwater into billowing clouds. The continual wind pushed the clouds northeast, where the settling ash eventually added elliptical aprons to the growing buttes.

Even by modern measures of time the eruptions lasted but a short while, a few months at most. In their wake twin volcanic cones—one 500 feet tall and the other 800 feet—stood as sentinels above the plain. The two buttes' center vents are marked by 300-foot-deep craters.

Because the Menan Buttes blocked the Henry's Fork channel, the river carved a new one farther east, compelling its confluence with the Snake to migrate south. Their combined currents also dredged a fresh riverbed, which today skirts around the southern butte's lower end.

SIGHTS TO SEE

Menan Buttes (A National Natural Landmark)

If coming from I-15 take Exit 143 and drive east 12 miles on Idaho State Road 33; if coming from US 20, take the Rexburg Exit and drive west 7.4 miles on Idaho State Road 33. From either direction turn south at the Sportsman Access for the Menan Buttes and drive 4.1 miles as the road climbs over the saddle separating the two cones.

To hike up the higher northern butte, turn right on the unmarked, steep dirt road leading 0.2 mile to a parking area. An easy although at times obscure trail leads to the rim. If you miss it, it's possible to scramble up from about anywhere. Before hiking into the crater or around the rim, take your bearings so you'll know where to descend to your vehicle.

The views of Henry's Fork and the Snake River Plain are well worth the effort. (Approaches to the south butte cross private land, so please request permission before hiking.)

When leaving: From the dirt road turnoff to the north butte, continue 0.8 mile to Twin Buttes Road. Go left for access to the Snake River. To return to Idaho State Road 33, turn right and drive four miles to an unnamed intersection; turn left and proceed another 1.1 miles to the highway.

Clark Fork River squeezed by the cliffs of Cabinet Gorge.

THE SPOKANE FLOODS

Where the Clark Fork River enters the eastern border of northern Idaho, Cabinet Gorge pinches the current into a narrow channel before letting it empty into Lake Pend Oreille. During the most recent ice age, glaciers inching down from Canada cloaked Idaho's panhandle beneath a white blanket. A bit upstream from the mouth of the Clark Fork, the compressed snow piled over a mile high, plugging the river at Cabinet Gorge. Behind it summer meltwater from Montana's glaciers formed the greatest ice-dammed lake ever recorded: Glacial Lake Missoula.

Eventually growing in area to the equivalent of three Rhode Islands, the lake's 500 cubic miles of water lapped at its glacial stopper. Then somewhere around 20,000 years ago Lake Missoula gnawed away the edges of its frozen dam.

The lighter, less dense ice popped out of the gorge as if it were a champagne cork. With nothing to hold back the lake, a mountain of water nearly 1.7 times as tall as the Empire State Building surged over the Sandpoint town site, down the Purcell Trench toward Coeur d'Alene and westward into Washington's Spokane River Valley.

Iceberg rafts—much like frozen surfboards riding a giant wave—carried boulders the size of school buses for hundreds of miles. In eastern Washington the torrent fanned over the countryside and scraped the earth to its basalt core. Today a barren scabland the size of Delaware offers silent testimony to the flood's power.

Striking the lower Snake, the cataclysm reversed the river's course. Yielding to the inland tide, the Snake recoiled, its current racing back upstream until it was once more in Idaho. At the state line, the surge divided. One part turned south, driving the Snake almost to within sight of Hells Canyon. Meanwhile, the other portion slammed into the Clearwater River. When the upstream momentum finally exhausted its energy, the lowlands where Lewiston now stands were submersed beneath 600 feet of water. Today the city rests on a terrace of sediment left behind when the flood receded.

During the flood's one- or two-day climax, the flow reached that of 2,300 modern Columbia Rivers. Within a few weeks, the equal of 62 Lake Meads scoured northern Idaho and the Columbia River Plateau before filling the Columbia River Gorge and then submerging what are now Portland, Oregon, and the Willamette Valley.

Eventually the water drained into the Pacific Ocean, but in its wake it left potholes, gravel bars, canyons, and the scars of dead waterfalls. Idaho's Lake Coeur d'Alene and Priest Lake owe their existence to the Spokane Floods.

Yes, floods. After the initial one, glaciers again choked Cabinet Gorge, allowing Lake Missoula to refill. Once more the ice cork popped and the cataract roared across the Idaho panhandle and on to the sea.

Geologists have counted 41 separate floods, each progressively smaller than the first one, which was 25,000 times larger than any ever recorded on the Mississippi River. That Spokane Flood was one of the greatest floods in the history of the world.

Cabinet Gorge

From Sandpoint drive east on Idaho State Road 200 for 30 miles and turn right at the sign for the Cabinet Gorge Dam Overlook. For much of the way the road parallels picturesque Lake Pond Oreille, Idaho's largest lake.

Fur trappers named Cabinet Gorge after the many nooks eroded in its canyon walls. In the early 1920s the Board on Geographic Names chose Clark Fork (in honor of William Clark of Lewis and Clark fame) for the river over names it had been known by in the past, such as Hell Gate, Silverbow, and Missoula. The Cabinet Gorge Dam, which was completed in 1952, holds back the Clark Fork River in a 24-mile-long reservoir, nearly all of which is in Montana.

THE SNAKE

A Mighty River with Many Names

In 1805 when William Clark reached the lower Snake River near present-day Lewiston, Idaho, he assumed the Snake and the Salmon River, which he'd termed the River of No Return when he saw it some weeks earlier, were one and the same. Indians had told him about a major river merging with the Salmon from the south, but Clark thought it was merely a tributary. Because he had already honored Meriwether Lewis, the co-commander of their Voyage of Discovery, by naming the Salmon after him, Clark applied Lewis's name to the lower Snake as well. Early 19th century cartographers eventually corrected Clark's error in geography by designating the Snake River as the Lewis Fork of the Columbia and the smaller Salmon as the North Branch of the Lewis.

When the Astorian trapping brigade leader Wilson Price Hunt saw the South Fork of the Snake in 1811, he dubbed it the Canoe River. Upon reaching the Snake's North Fork, Hunt christened it Henry's Fork, for the trapper Andrew Henry, who had wintered beside it several months before. After Hunt's men abandoned their boat-descent of the Snake at the falls of Caldron Linn, they labeled the waterway the Mad River. Henry's Fork was the only name that stuck.

Collectively the Shoshones called themselves *Neme*, meaning the people; however, their sign was the snake, and they used its writhing motion to greet strangers. Some bands dubbed their majestic river *Biavahünu*, while others called it *Pohogawa*, which translates into River of the Sage Plain. Fur trappers such as William Sublette and Jedediah Smith referred to the Shoshones as the Snake Indians and substituted the name Snake River for Lewis Fork of the Columbia.

After gazing at the farms of Magic Valley, made green by

View from Sinker Butte: Swan Falls Dam holding back the Snake River.

the Snake's liquid treasure, a few modern writers have tagged the river the Nile of Idaho.

By whatever name, the Snake River owes its existence to the ice ages. Although Idaho shows evidence of only two glacial periods, some geologists think the state may have undergone many more. Although the latest one reached its zenith 15,000 years ago, the first may have formed two or three million years earlier.

During each of the ice ages, glaciers blanketed the state's panhandle and sculpted the mountains into jagged pinnacles. On the Snake River Plain, the heavy winter snows melted during the brief, rainy summers. In the warm, interglacial periods, the thawing ice released vast torrents. Valleys, such as Swan and Teton, saw the runoff erode new streambeds as it raced relentlessly downhill.

On the eastern Snake River Plain, the water searched out the low ground where the south-slopping basalt landscape disappeared under the north-reaching alluvial deposits from mountain ranges such as the Portneufs and Albions. Because the Snake River Plain also drops elevation from east to west, the water rushed toward present-day Mountain Home and Boise, where it pooled in a vast chain of lakes, known collectively as Lake Idaho.

During this time one of the lake's outlets was a minor branch of the Salmon River. This predecessor of the Snake began eroding its way upstream, eventually eating through Lake Idaho's northern rim. About one million years ago the lake gushed from its boundary, enlarging the Snake's channel and carving Hells Canyon.

With each succeeding ice age the Snake cut its channel ever deeper. By the end of the most recent ice age, 10,000 years ago, the Snake had become a mighty river.

Today the Snake meanders 1,110 miles, descending over 8,500 feet from the mountains of Yellowstone National Park to its confluence with the Columbia River near Kennewick, Washington. In Hells Canyon it roils through the nation's deepest gorge. At 7,900 feet, Hells Canyon is one-third mile deeper than the Grand Canyon. From headwaters to mouth, the Snake drains 3.7% of the total land area of the lower 48 states. Rated by volume of water carried, it is America's sixth largest river; by length, her tenth longest. The Snake's annual flow could fill Hoover Dam's Lake Mead and have enough left over to flood every farm on the Snake River Plain to a depth of two feet.

Although it's 340 miles shorter than the Colorado River, the Snake carries double the amount of water. Yet each summer at Milner Dam, west of Burley, virtually the entire river is drained into the irrigation canals of the Magic Valley. Then below Twin Falls, the river miraculously refills, fed first by the Thousand Springs of the Snake River Plain Aquifer and later by rivers such as the Malad, Bruneau, and Boise.

The Snake has witnessed some of the greatest floods the world has ever known. The Spokane Flood, 20,000 years ago, released a wall of water across northern Idaho, creating Lake Coeur d'Alene before washing away eastern Washington's topsoil. Striking the Snake at its mouth, this surge raced upstream, reversing the river's course and submerging the Lewiston town-site under 600 feet of water. In its wake lay a terrace of sediment on which the city now stands.

Then 14,500 years ago, the top 300 feet of ancient Lake Bonneville hurdled through the Snake's gorges. In some places the flood deposited gravel flats like the ones Burley and Rupert are built on, and in others it eroded alcoves such as the Blue Lakes Complex of Twin Falls, where golfers now attempt to break par.

Modern man has sought to tame the Snake River by sectioning it with dams. Turbines at these hydroelectric facilities generate power for four states. Every summer thousands of acres of thirsty Idaho farmland are nurtured by endless miles of irrigation ditches, all fed by the Snake. Over one-half million Idahoans—50 percent of the state—live on the 100-mile-wide ribbon of land that straddles the Snake's channel.

Without the Snake River, southern Idaho wouldn't enjoy the bounty it has today. Still, this wealth comes at a price.

Salmon no longer spawn within sight of Shoshone Falls. Pesticide-laden silt is slowly choking the reservoirs. And between Murtaugh and Upper Salmon Falls, algae are suffocating the fish and other aquatic animals.

Dams, such as Swan Falls and Brownlee, have halted the

salmon's migration, whereas Milner so reduces the downstream flow, the river is unable to flush its algae-breeding pollutants.

The Snake is a great river, but some Idahoans think the waterway is being asked to do too much. Its plight has set environmentalists against farmers, rafters against jet boaters, and fishermen against the power authorities.

The Snake's problems are too complex for the quick fixes that usually favor one constituency while threatening the values or livelihood of another. There are no easy answers. Nonetheless, solutions must be found before Idaho loves the Snake River to death.

Swan Falls Dam

From I-84 Exit 44 west of Boise, drive eight miles south on Idaho State Road 69 to Kuna. At the Kuna Ward LDS Church where the road curves sharply right, continue straight 20 yards and turn left on Swan Falls Road. The Dam is 21 miles south in the Snake River Birds of Prey National Conservation Area. Be sure to watch for raptors gliding on the air currents and for the numerous prairie dogs, which make up the birds' diet.

A footbridge across the dam leads to hiking and mountain biking trails. Sinker Butte (the high point south of the river; elevation 3,421 feet) offers stunning views of the Snake River Plain and Owyhee Mountains.

THE BONNEVILLE FLOOD

Imagine an ancient Native American standing on the south rim of the Snake River Canyon near present-day Twin Falls. A faint roar catches his ear. Glancing down at the water, he notices its churning waves battering the canyon's sides.

The sound amplifies, rumbling with the throaty clamor of a thunderstorm. Beneath the onlooker's feet the earth vibrates as if it were the skin of bass drum.

Suddenly, a surge of brown froth bursts around the distant bend. It hits the outside cliff and ricochets across the chasm. Behind the foam, driving it, hurling it at breakneck speed, rushes a boiling caldron.

Striking the narrows, the water piles up as north of the canyon another torrent barrels across the lava plain toward the rim and then plunges over in a sweeping cataract. In the gorge the river climbs the shadowed walls to the brim and overflows.

During the last ice age Idaho's panhandle slept under a blanket of snow. Glaciers scooped 1,000 feet of sediment from Lake Pend Oreille and choked the Purcell Trench toward Rathdrum. In the Bitterroot and Sawtooth ranges, ice carved the mountains into precipitous pinnacles and knife-edged arêtes.

But on the Snake River Plain and in the valleys of northern Utah, the heavy winter snows melted during the brief, rainy summers. Much of this water collected in a vast basin known as Lake Bonneville.

Having no outlet through which to drain, Lake Bonneville expanded for 13,000 years until it covered 20,000 square miles of northern Utah and eastern Nevada. In time its tentacles reached into southeastern Idaho. What is now Salt Lake City sat beneath

Perrine Bridge shadow on the Snake River, where the waters of the Bonneville Flood once filled the canyon to the brim.

800 feet of water. In Idaho, the hay fields near Franklin and Preston lay submerged, as did I-15 east of Woodruff and parts of the Curlew Valley.

At Idaho's Red Rock Pass, the lake's lowest boundary, the waves eventually spilled over the shoreline. For the next five centuries Lake Bonneville ceased to grow as its annual rainfall was siphoned off by a northern outlet known today as Marsh Creek. Then in a geologic blink of an eye 14,500 years ago, the stream ate through its rock boundary and flushed away the underlying alluvium dam.

Water began pouring down Marsh Creek to the Portneuf River and into the Snake. As more and more rock and clay were washed away, the deluge grew from a torrent to a flood. It took nearly a month for the top 300 feet of Lake Bonneville to empty, and in that time the equivalent of three Amazon Rivers swept across the Snake River Plain.

The surging water rolled and polished boulders the size of Smart Cars and MINI Coopers. Near Massacre Rocks State Park, the flood flushed away a basalt dam that had built a prehistoric lake where the American Falls Reservoir now stands.

Upstream from the Murtaugh narrows, the Snake River backed up until overflowing its northern flank. The overflow then hurdled west, carving the Eden Channel and washing the loess from the underlying basalt. The resulting landscape resembled a blackened scab. When the floodwaters reached Twin Falls, they poured back into the main Snake River canyon and in the process created the Blue Lakes complex.

Massive whirlpools sucked away the streambed beneath bands of hard volcanic rock, creating spectacular drops such as Shoshone Falls. Every constricted bend along the entire Snake River gorge bunched the water to overflowing. At Rock Creek, at Swan Falls, at Pittsburg Landing and elsewhere over the length of the lower Snake River, as the ponding flood awaited its release, its burden of gravel and sand was deposited in mile-long, 100-foot-high bars such as the ones white water rafters now picnic on in Hells Canyon.

Although the peak discharge lasted only a few weeks, Lake

Bonneville continued draining for ten months. By the time it stopped, it had lost enough water to fill Lake Michigan.

When the ice age ended and the land became more arid, the remaining water began evaporating. Today the Great Salt Lake is all that is left. Yet if the world enters another ice age, Lake Bonneville's basin could once more fill. But without the eroded lip of Red Rock Pass, Lake Bonneville will never again equal its former majesty.

Car-size boulder at Massacre Rocks State Park. Stones even larger than this were rolled and polished by the Bonneville Flood.

SIGHTS TO SEE

Massacre Rocks State Park (containing boulders rounded by the Bonneville Flood)

Take I-86 Exit 28 approximately 10 miles southwest of American Falls and follow the signs.

Perrine Bridge Snake River Overlook (with views of the Blue Lakes cataract complex)

Located off U.S. 93 just north of Twin Falls.

Red Rock Pass (4,785 feet of elevation) and Red Rock Pass Geologic Monument

Located alongside U.S. 91 about four miles north of Swan Lake.

Part Two

A PEOPLE FORGED BY COURAGE

SACAJAWEA'S
Idaho Homecoming

In early August 1805 the Voyage of Discovery was in its second year. Captains Meriwether Lewis and William Clark had already explored the Missouri River to the Three Forks, where the Jefferson, Madison, and Gallatin Rivers merge. Now as their men laboriously dragged their canoes through the rocky shallows of the Beaverhead River (north of Dillon, Montana), the captains looked forward to reaching the Missouri's headwaters and cresting the Continental Divide.

On August 8 as the expedition set up its evening camp, Sacajawea, the Shoshone wife of the interpreter Toussaint Charbonneau, excitedly pointed at a distant hill, calling it the Beaver's Head. She remembered it from her childhood, before her capture by a Hidatsa war party. She said her people spent their summers in a valley to the west. Motioning toward the Beaverhead Mountains, she told Lewis and Clark about a pass the Shoshones used when going to hunt buffalo. She felt certain her tribe was camped somewhere beyond.

Lewis and Clark knew they must find Indians. The expedition had to have horses, or it would be unable to transport its supplies over the mountains.

The following morning Lewis and three other men left the main party, intending to cross the Bitterroot Range and locate the Shoshones. Clark was to continue up the Beaverhead River with the expedition's canoes.

On August 12 Lewis climbed Lemhi Pass and entered what would become Idaho. That afternoon he had his first drink from a creek whose waters eventually flowed to the Pacific Ocean.

The next day Lewis descended into the Lemhi Valley. Although he spotted several Indians, they ran off when he tried to

Agency Creek Road winding its way down from Lemhi Pass.

approach. Heading north along the Lemhi River, he finally came on three women who were too frightened to flee. Lewis gave the women presents, persuading them to lead him to their home. They took him two miles farther when 60 Shoshone warriors came galloping to the women's rescue.

After learning the women were unharmed, Chief Cameahwait invited the Americans to the Shoshones' camp (near Tendoy, Idaho). Lewis soon prevailed upon the chief and some of his band to accompany him back over Lemhi Pass to where Clark and the rest of the party were waiting. As an inducement, Lewis said the expedition included a young Shoshone woman who'd been taken captive as a girl.

When the Shoshones reached the Americans' main body, Sacajawea began sucking her fingers, a sign the Indians were members of her tribe. To her immense joy she discovered a woman who she'd been friends with as a child. The Hidatsas had stolen them at the same time, and Sacajawea's friend had escaped by leaping through a stream.

While the two women renewed their bond, Lewis and Clark began to parley with Chief Cameahwait. After smoking a ceremonial pipe, the captains sent for Sacajawea. When she entered the tent where they were meeting, she recognized the chief as her brother. Overcome by her emotions, the young woman embraced him as she wept tears of happiness.

During the next three days Captain Clark, Sacajawea, Charbonneau, and 11 other members of the expedition accompanied the Shoshones over Lemhi Pass to their camp in the Lemhi Valley. Taking a native guide, Clark continued to the Salmon River, hoping it would provide a water passage to the coast. He was soon disappointed. Several miles west of present-day North Fork, Idaho, he judged the Salmon unrunnable, deeming it a "river of no return."

Meanwhile at the Shoshones' camp, Sacajawea met a warrior who she'd been promised to when she was a girl. To her relief, the brave renounced his claim because she had borne Charbonneau a son.

Escorted by 50 mounted Shoshones, Sacajawea and Charboneau re-crossed Lemhi Pass into Montana, where the expedition's main body was caching its canoes and surplus stores. After ordering the remaining baggage packed on the Indians' ponies, Lewis led the Voyage of Discovery into Idaho to join up with Clark. On August 26 Sacajawea topped Lemhi Pass for the last time.

Lemhi Pass (7,339 ft.; a National Historic Landmark and part of the Lewis and Clark National Back Country Byway)

From Tendoy on Idaho State Road 28 (20 miles south of Salmon and 140 miles northwest of Idaho Falls) turn east on Agency Creek Road for 0.1 mile. At the T turn left and follow the Back Country Byway signs 27 miles to Lemhi Pass.

From the pass, it's 0.2 miles to the Sacajawea Memorial Campground (tents only) and the Laura Tolman Wild Flower Trail. To return to State Road 28, descend Agency Creek Road 12.2 miles to Tendoy. Along the way watch for the historical sign marking where on August 12, 1805, Meriwether Lewis spent his first night in Idaho.

Although these gravel roads are suitable for automobiles, **trailers and buses are not advised**. The roads are usually closed by snow from November to June.

Beaverhead Mountains Scenic Loop

From Lemhi Pass follow Montana Forest Road 324 east 12.1 miles to Montana State Highway 324. Turn right and in 12.3 miles cross back into Idaho at Bannock Pass (7,485 ft.), where the road becomes Idaho State Road 29. Descend 13.8 miles to Idaho State Road 28 in Leadore.

DAVID THOMPSON

The Peripatetic Map Maker

Nearly blind, old David Thompson was so broke he sold his surveying instruments and heavy winter coat. Several years before, he had tried selling the story of his adventure's to Washington Irving, but the noted American writer and he couldn't come to terms. Then on February 16, 1857, just outside Montreal, Quebec, David Thompson died: a forgotten pauper.

Yet in his lifetime Thompson had discovered the headwaters of the Mississippi River. He made the first complete reconnaissance of the Columbia. He surveyed much of the western boundary between the United States and Canada. He wrote 39 journals and drew countless maps. And as chief topographer of the North West Company of Montreal, he rode, canoed, and walked nearly 55,000 miles, many of them in Idaho.

Though Thompson was only 14 years old in 1784 when he sailed from England to Canada, he'd already been apprenticed to the Hudson's Bay Company. For the next 13 years the young Welshman worked at various posts, learning the fur trade and surveying. Finding his interest lay in geography instead of commerce, Thompson grew restless when the company sought to discourage him from drawing maps.

In 1797 Thompson quit the Hudson's Bay Company and joined its chief rival, the North West Company. During the next 15 years, he busied himself sorting out the tangled rivers that drained the firm's vast fur empire. One by one the blank sections on the company's maps disappeared.

Thompson didn't confine his curiosity to surveys. Little in the natural world escaped his attention. He studied everything from star constellations to birds, and he went so far as to allow mosquitoes to feed on his arm while he examined their behavior through a magnifying glass. And one winter he deduced that the color of a person's eyes determined his sensitivity to snow blindness.

A religious man, Thompson forswore tobacco, profanity, and whiskey. At evening campfires he often read the Bible in French to his illiterate voyageurs. And he worked tirelessly to prevent his traders from giving liquor to the Indians.

In 1808 Thompson first set foot in Idaho, coming down the Kootenai River. In September the following year, he established Kullyspell House on a jut of land in Lake Pend Oreille. Intended for the Colville, Spokane, Coeur d'Alene, and Flathead Indian trade, this single-room log post lasted but one year until harassment by Blackfoot war parties closed its doors. Although it was owned by a Canadian company, Kullyspell House was the first trading post in Idaho.

During 1811 and 1812 Thompson's explorations culminated in the first complete survey of the Columbia River. He not only mapped it from source to mouth, but he also charted many of the Columbia's tributaries. Side surveys took him 56 miles up the Snake River as well as along the banks of the Clark Fork and Pend Oreille Rivers.

Thompson last came through Idaho in early spring 1812 on his way to Quebec. Soon after reaching Montreal, he resigned from the North West Company. Although he continued working as a surveyor, his fortunes steadily declined until his death.

Thompson's maps remain his crowning achievement. One, measuring 10 feet long, displayed the 1.5 million square miles he had explored. Considered too valuable to be seen by the North West Company's competitors, it hung in a locked room at Fort William (on the north shore of Lake Superior), visible to no one except the company's partners.

Memorial to one of North America's greatest cartographers: David Thompson.

David Thompson's Memorial

Drive 16 miles east from Sandpoint on Idaho State Road 200, turning north (left) at the sign for Hope. Follow this road through Hope for 1.2 miles. The monument is on the right, just inside East Hope.

Kullyspell House was located on Memaloose Point, a small peninsula in Lake Pend Oreille, just off Idaho State Road 200 near Hope. According to locals, the actual site has been under water for years, ever since dams raised the elevation of the lake.

McBRIDE
1810

FORT HENRY

The Bonneville Museum in downtown Idaho Falls displays a curious rock that's chiseled with five names, a cross, and the date 1810. The top name is A. Henry.

In 1917 Hazen Hawkes uncovered this rock on his family's farm alongside Conant Creek, several miles southeast of Marysville. The location was the site of Camp Henry.

Andrew Henry came west from St. Louis in 1809, co-commanding a Missouri Fur Company trapping brigade. Where the Madison, Jefferson, and Gallatin Rivers converge—the Three Forks of the Missouri—he and his mountain men built a fort and started emptying the streams of beaver. Just when they began to enjoy a bountiful harvest, Blackfoot warriors descended intent on ridding their country of white interlopers.

By the next June Henry had read over eight graves, including that of George Drouillard, who first saw this country with Lewis and Clark.

Unable to fight the Blackfeet and take fur too, Henry abandoned the Three Forks but not the mountains. Near the Madison's headwaters, he and a handful of volunteers crossed the Continental Divide into Idaho. A few nights later while camped beside what is now Henry's Lake, he learned he hadn't left his Indian problems in Montana. A party of Crows stole most of his company's horses.

The trappers trudged south with their gear packed on the few mounts the Crows hadn't taken. Their route followed a fork of the Snake River that within another year would also carry Henry's name. On the Egin Bench north of present-day Rexburg, half of his men refused to go farther. Henry had no choice but to leave them, advising them to construct a shelter for the coming winter.

The Camp Henry 1810 stone marker with the names of Andrew Henry, John Hoback, P. McBride, and B. Jackson is on display at the Bonneville County Museum in Idaho Falls.

Their intended quarters proved inauspicious, since *egin* is the Shoshone word for cold.

Taking John Hoback, L. Cather, P. McBride, and B. Jackson, Andrew Henry headed up the Falls River, and then turned onto Conant Creek. At what would eventually become the Hawkes's farm, the five men established Camp Henry, and one of them etched their names on a stone marker.

By the time the encroaching ice ended the trapping season, the small company had collected a good catch of pelts. Shortly after the New Year, everyone gathered on Egin Bench to wait out the snow. The men Henry left there the previous fall had built a few crude log huts.

Winter proved harder on spirit than body. Before the snowdrifts from the last blizzard melted, one of the men snapped. Taking his rifle, he deserted. Although Henry often saw him watching the huts from afar, nothing could induce the crazed trapper to return.

Following the spring thaw, Henry and his remaining men loaded their horses with 40 packs of beaver and climbed back over the Divide. The deranged deserter stayed behind.

Andrew Henry led another fur brigade to the mountains in 1822, but he never again set foot in Idaho. The log cabins his men built beside Henry's Fork of the Snake River have come to be known as Fort Henry, America's first trading post west of the Continental Divide.

Fort Henry: Broken monument marking the site of Fort Henry.

FORT HENRY

SIGHTS TO SEE

Bonneville County Museum

Located at the intersection of Elm and N. Eastern Avenues in Idaho Falls.

Site of Fort Henry

From the North Rexburg exit of US 20, turn north on the Salem-Parker Road (also called N. Salem Road and 1900 E. Road). After 4.4 miles come to the defaced Fort Henry Monument 100 yards south of Henry's Fork River. The fort sat in the bottomland one-third mile east.

CALDRON LINN
and the Astorians

In 1810 Wilson Price Hunt journeyed west from St. Louis, leading a Pacific Fur Company overland expedition toward the mouth of the Columbia River. Hunt was a junior partner in the company, which was a tiny fiefdom within John Jacob Astor's fur empire that also included the mighty American Fur Company.

Astor had grand plans. He'd already dispatched the 290-ton sailing ship *Tonquin* around Cape Horn to establish a trading post on the Oregon coast. The facility was to be named Fort Astoria. Now, Hunt's 62-man force was bringing the muscle to harvest the country's beaver. Trappers in Hunt's party would glean the streams and ponds of their pelts. Astor's ships would then take the furs to China, trade them for tea and silk, and sail the valuable cargo to New York to be sold. The ships would then return to Fort Astoria with more supplies. If everything worked out as Astor had planned it, the cycle of trade could be continually repeated.

In 1811 Hunt entered Idaho via Teton Pass. In early October his expedition reached the North Fork of the Snake River, a few miles north of present-day Rexburg. The young commander named the waterway Henry's Fork after Andrew Henry, who'd wintered beside it the previous year. Eleven days later Hunt left his horses with a band of Shoshones and started downriver in 15 dugout canoes his men had hewn from cottonwoods.

Near the Menan Buttes, where Henry's Fork converges with the South Fork of the Snake River, the quicker current of the combined streams portended trouble. At American Falls the company portaged. A bit below the future site of Milner Dam one of the canoes struck a boulder and flipped, drowning Antoine Clappine. Ramsay Crooks, the party's deputy commander, and four other Astorians were riding with Clappine and barely escaped with their lives.

A few miles later the rowers again pulled into shore, alerted by frantic signals from the lead boat. Ahead the river gained speed as it rushed toward a loud roar. Leaving their canoes, Hunt and his men tramped through the sagebrush that dotted the sandy bottomland.

A short distance from where they had beached, the volcanic walls pinched the Snake into a constricted flume. The bunched water shot through the gap as if sluiced down a mountain. Surging over a ledge, the river plunged into a seething basin of green frothy boils.

An Astorian named Robert Stuart later confided to his diary that "Hecate's caldron was never half so agitated when vomiting even the most diabolical spells, as is this Linn." From Stuart's entry, this narrowest and most southern portion of the Snake River took its name: Caldron Linn.

Wondering what other surprises the Snake could be holding, Hunt dispatched scouts. The reconnaissance cost several days and more wrecked canoes. Even worse, its conclusion was disheartening. The river wasn't navigable.

Hunt sent Crooks and a few men to retrieve their horses from the Shoshones. In the meantime, he and the remainder of the party awaited their return near Caldron Linn. When some of his group asked permission to press on to Fort Astoria on foot, the commander grudgingly allowed them to try.

Fearful lest the expedition be overtaken by winter, Crooks soon abandoned his quest for the horses and returned to Caldron Linn. Needing to move, Hunt cached everything that couldn't be carried and on November 9 began walking to the Oregon coast.

Crooks and 18 men followed the Snake's left shore, while Hunt led the balance of the expedition down the right. For the next two months the parties struggled across Idaho in the face of deteriorating weather. Desperately in want of food and horses, they veered away from the Snake, hoping to locate friendly Indians. At the Weiser River Hunt met a band of Indians which traded him a couple of ponies, some dried salmon, and most important, the services of a native guide.

After reuniting with Crooks' group, Hunt left the deputy leader and five others—who were now too exhausted to travel—in the care of some friendly Shoshones. Beyond the Snake River, the expedition headed over the Blue Mountains into the lush valleys of Oregon. For weeks on end, the weary march continued, broken only by an occasional rest with an amicable tribe.

On January 21, 1812, the company reached the Columbia River. Below The Dalles, the men again took to canoes, finally arriving at Fort Astoria on February 15. Here, Hunt met those men he'd permitted to leave Caldron Linn ahead of the main body in early November. They had beaten him by a month.

On May 11 Crooks, too, joined his companions at the Pacific Fur Company trading post, having regained his health among the Shoshones.

Caldron Linn—the southern-most point on the Snake River, where lava cliffs churn the current into a foaming brew.

Caldron Linn (also known as Star Falls)

Drive 22 miles west from Burley on US 30 and turn north toward Murtaugh on 4500 East Road. After 1.2 miles swing right into the village of Murtaugh for another 0.4 mile. Cross the railroad tracks, go through several jogs, and in 0.7 mile turn left at a T. Drive 1.6 miles, crossing the Snake River and then turn right on 1500 S and in one mile go right on 2000 E. In 0.7 mile you'll come to a steep, rough descent leading to the river. **Walk this unless you have a high-clearance, four-wheel-drive vehicle**.

From the flats near the river, a short trail leads to Caldron Linn and its numerous overlooks. At the narrowest point, the gorge is but 40 feet wide. **There are no handrails, so please use care especially if accompanying children**.

Teton Pass (8,431 ft.)

Drive east from Victor on Idaho State Road 33, which becomes Wyoming State Highway 22 at the state line. The highway crosses Teton Pass about eight miles east of the Wyoming line.

THE BATTLE
of Pierre's Hole

"Come a runnin' boys! Indian attack! Old Milt needs your help!"

On July 18, 1832, the frenzied cry shattered the rendezvous. The mountain men's annual summer celebration was winding to a close in Pierre's Hole, now picturesque Teton Valley near Driggs. The horse races, shooting contests, pageantry, and camaraderie had ended. During the coming months of freezing streams, hair-raising danger, and mind-numbing isolation, the memory of this year's rendezvous and the anticipation of the next would be the trappers' only solace.

As the riders shouted their call to arms, the buckskin-clad men grabbed their rifles and saddles. Many blinked bloodshot eyes, attempting to rid the cobwebs from brains dulled by the river-water-diluted alcohol Bill Sublette sold as whiskey.

The day before, Henry Fraeb and Bill's brother, Milton Sublette, had moved their Rocky Mountain Fur Company trapping brigades a few miles south, planning an early start after everyone shed his hangover. This morning a couple of hours after daybreak, they encountered a large band of Gros Ventres.

Generations earlier, the Gros Ventres had migrated north to present-day Montana where they became allies with the powerful Blackfoot confederation. Every few years since then, the Gros Ventres had ridden south to visit their cousins, the Arapahos. In the summer of 1832, the Gros Ventres were returning home from such a visit when they sighted the fur brigades.

The whites and Indians halted several hundred yards apart in order to size each other up. Seeing a Gros Ventre chief come forward to parley, Milt Sublette dispatched a Flathead brave who was a member of the brigade and Antoine Godin, who spoke the Gros Ventres' tongue. Instead of talking to the chief, the two emissaries shot him and lifted his scalp.

After a moment of disbelief, the Gros Ventres withdrew to a streambed and began piling deadfall and brush into a breastwork. Meanwhile, Milt Sublette sent riders to alert the rendezvous.

Soon reinforcements arrived, including Milt's brother. Seeing the trappers and allied Nez Perce and Flathead warriors milling about in an undisciplined horde, Bill Sublette took charge. He organized about 30 friendly Indians and a like number of mountain men into an attack force and led them forward. As the makeshift army came within range of the stronghold, the Gros Ventres greeted them with a withering barrage.

Bill's fighters dove for cover and began answering the Gros Ventres' fire. All day the two sides exchanged shots. When Bill rose up for a better look, a musket ball smashed into his arm. Unwilling to be carried to the rear, he insisted his men prop him against a cottonwood so he could continue directing the battle.

In the late afternoon a Gros Ventre brave shouted that many more of their tribe would soon come to their aid. Although it wasn't true, within minutes a mistranslation of the threat escalated into "Hundreds of warriors are raiding the rendezvous!"

In their dash to the fight, the mountain men had left behind their Indian wives and children as well as the stores needed for the coming year and the bales of valuable beaver pelts Bill Sublette's traders had acquired during the raucous celebration. Panic quickly rolled over the brigades. Even Bill was affected.

Wheeling about like a school of jittery fish, the rattled army raced back to the rendezvous. Barely a dozen men stayed to cover the Gros Ventres. Near twilight the trappers sheepishly returned, having found their camp as peaceful as a Sunday picnic.

At dawn Bill Sublette sought to renew the attack, but the Gros Ventres had crept away during the night. The Battle of Pierre's Hole was over. Five trappers and seven of their Indian allies were dead. No one knows how many casualties the Gros Ventres carried off.

The Battle of Pierre's Hole was the largest armed confrontation between Native Americans and trappers during the entire the mountain man era.

Pierre's Hole (valleys are holes in mountain man lexicon)

Named for the Iroquois fur trapper Pierre Tevanitagon, this picturesque valley is located in Teton County just west of the Wyoming state line. Now called the Teton Basin, Pierre's Hole is cut by Idaho State Road 33. The Teton River, which drains the basin, was once known as Pierre's River.

The 1832 rendezvous with its trapping brigades, friendly Indian camps, and grazing fields for the attendees' many horses occupied several acres of the Teton Basin near Driggs. Although no one is certain, some historians place the battle site beside Trail Creek, 1½ miles northwest of Victor.

Pastoral Teton Basin beneath the towering Tetons, known by the mountain men as Pierre's Hole. During the 1832 rendezvous the tranquility of this lovely valley was shattered by a deadly battle.

FORT HALL'S
Cambridge Ice Cutter

"Gentlemen, I will yet roll a stone into your garden that you will never be able to get out."

In June 1834 on Ham's Fork (a river in name only) in the southwest corner of present-day Wyoming, Nathaniel Jarvis Wyeth issued his famous threat. As the angry Wyeth strode away from Tom Fitzpatrick's and Jim Bridger's rendezvous camp, the two Rocky Mountain Fur Company partners had no idea the Cambridge, Massachusetts, ice cutter would soon build a trading post in the midst of their fur empire.

Today a small monument marks Fort Hall's location alongside the Snake River, a few miles upstream from the American Falls Reservoir. The land belongs to the Bannock and Shoshone tribes.

Wyeth had come to the mountains two years earlier, wanting to make his fortune in beaver pelts. Compared to his previous occupation of cutting and selling ice from the pond beside his home near Harvard College, the life of a fur trader must have seemed exciting. Besides, John Jacob Astor and General William Ashley had grown rich on fur, so why not him?

Wyeth's first venture failed when the supply ship he sent around Cape Horn to meet him on the Oregon coast sank. In 1833 he returned to Massachusetts in company with Milt Sublette, also a partner in the Rocky Mountain Fur Company. Sublette was going east to seek medical treatment for his diseased foot.

During the journey Sublette contracted for Wyeth to furnish the Rocky Mountain Fur Company with supplies at the next rendezvous. With that agreement in hand, Wyeth persuaded several Boston investors to provide the financial backing.

On April 28, 1834, the Cambridge ice cutter led his pack train west from Independence, Missouri. Milt Sublette began the journey with him but soon turned back. His foot had grown worse.

Wyeth drove his men and mules relentlessly as they pushed

along the Platte River. He needed to hurry, because hard on his heels rode Milt's brother, Bill Sublette. Bill had outfitted the Rocky Mountain Fur Company since its beginning, and he had no intention abandoning the lucrative trade to an eastern upstart. Thirteen days out from Independence, Bill Sublette's caravan edged into the lead, an advantage it never relinquished.

By the time Wyeth crossed trails with Tom Fitzpatrick's brigade on the Green River, Bill Sublette had already secured the Rocky Mountain Fur Company's trade. Fitzpatrick, the firm's managing partner, repudiated the contract Wyeth had made with Milt Sublette, leaving Wyeth stuck with several thousand dollars' worth of unsold stores.

Instead of returning to Massachusetts with nothing to show for his and his backers' investment, Wyeth decided to build a trading post on the Snake River and barter with the local Indians. Construction began Tuesday, July 15, and was completed three weeks later. Named for Henry Hall, one of Wyeth's investors, Fort Hall became an instant thorn in the side of the Hudson's Bay Company, which counted the Snake River drainage as part of its vast Columbia Department that was headquartered at Fort Vancouver (across the Columbia River from present-day Portland, Oregon). The British fur-trading monopoly soon countered with a post of its own: Fort Boise.

Although Wyeth tried, he couldn't compete with the English on one side and the American fur companies on the other. Broke, he returned to his Cambridge ice business in 1836, having agreed to sell Fort Hall to the Hudson's Bay Company.

During the 1840s and early 1850s, Wyeth's former trading post became an important rest stop for thousands of families on the Oregon Trail. By the mid-1850s declining emigration and bypasses such as Hudspeth's Cutoff had so reduced the numbers of wagons passing the fort that it was no longer profitable. In 1856 the Hudson's Bay Company finally closed its gates.

Fort Hall

A reproduction of the trading post is located in Pocatello's Ross Park. Take I-15 Exit 67 to 5th Ave. North. Turn left on Fredregill and then go left again on 4th Ave. and make an immediate right on Ave. of Chiefs.

The original fort sat beside the Snake River in Fort Hall Bottoms west-southwest of Fort Hall village and US 91. Since the grounds are on the Fort Hall Indian Reservation, those wishing to visit the site must secure a permit from the Shoshone-Bannock Tribal Council.

Fort Hall as it looked when owned by the Hudson's Bay Company.

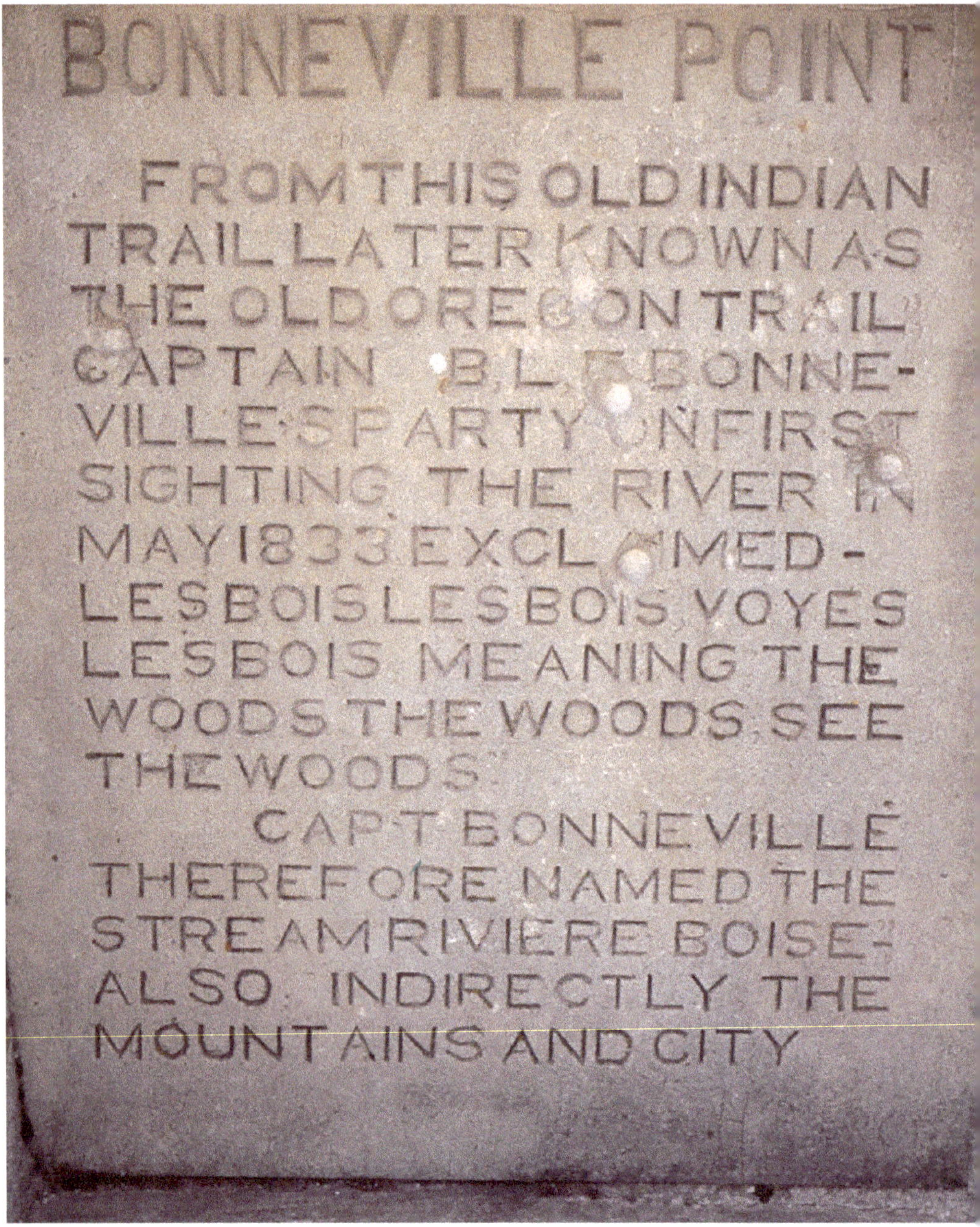

BONNEVILLE POINT

FROM THIS OLD INDIAN
TRAIL LATER KNOWN AS
THE OLD OREGON TRAIL"
CAPTAIN B.L.E. BONNE-
VILLE'S PARTY ON FIRST
SIGHTING THE RIVER IN
MAY 1833 EXCLAIMED-
LES BOIS LES BOIS VOYES
LES BOIS MEANING THE
WOODS THE WOODS SEE
THE WOODS"
CAPT BONNEVILLE
THEREFORE NAMED THE
STREAM RIVIERE BOISE-
ALSO INDIRECTLY THE
MOUNTAINS AND CITY

Historical marker at Bonneville Point.

AN AMERICAN PATRIOT

Benjamin Louis Eulalie de Bonneville

B*onneville County; Bonneville Peak; Bonneville Flood; Bonneville Dam; Bonneville Power Authority; Bonneville Salt Flats; the Pontiac Bonneville...*

The name Bonneville has been appended to much of our state and our nation. Idaho Falls has the Bonneville Museum. At Massacre Rocks State Park, east of Burley, are "melon" boulders, which were rounded and polished by the Bonneville Flood. Southeast of Pocatello stands Bonneville Peak. At 9,271 feet, it's the tallest point in the Portneuf Range.

Who was this man whose name not only marks so many features of the intermountain west but also embellishes a once-popular automobile?

Immigrant, West Point Cadet, Soldier, Fur Trapper, Patriot: During his life, Benjamin Louis Eulalie de Bonneville wore each of these titles.

He was born in France in 1796 and came to the United States as a young child. At 17 he won an appointment to the U.S. Military Academy, and in 1815 he received his commission. Bonneville's early Army career revealed nothing that would lead to his name being bestowed with the abandon of a politician's promises.

Then in 1831 his superiors granted him a two-year leave to take a trapping expedition to the Rocky Mountains. Some historians speculate that he went as a spy, that he was sent to gather information about the British, who shared joint occupancy of the country we now call Washington, Oregon, western Wyoming and Idaho. In any case, the need to arrange non-government financing for his venture and to pull together the necessary provisions delayed his departure until spring 1832.

For over three years Bonneville's trappers emptied the streams and ponds of their beaver. In Idaho his mountain men camped beside the Bear River and the Salmon. And they also trudged across the arid Snake River Plain. Hot and thirsty when they crested a hill overlooking present-day Boise, they saw in the distance a river, its banks lush with green-leafed trees. Some legends say it was here at Bonneville Point that Bonneville's French-speaking trappers gave our state capital and its river their name: "*Les bois, les bois. Voyes les bois!*" ("The woods, the woods. See the woods!")

After returning to the East Coast nearly two years beyond his authorized leave, Bonneville learned the Army had dropped him from its rolls. For the next 12 months as he doggedly sought reinstatement, he wrote about his western travels and eventually sold the unpolished manuscript to Washington Irving.

When the noted author rewrote and published the work as *The Adventures of Captain Bonneville,* the book became an instant success. Bonneville became a national hero, nearly on par with Lewis and Clark, and his name became synonymous with enterprise and daring.

Meanwhile the Army relented and again allowed Bonneville to don a soldier's uniform. In Florida he led troops against the Seminole Indians. During the Mexican War, he waded ashore at Vera Cruz, fought at Mexico City, and was wounded by grapeshot at Churubusco. And in the 1850s he battled the Apaches and Navahos in the southwest.

The Civil War found Bonneville too old for combat. Still he played his part, serving as Superintendent of Recruiting in St. Louis. Shortly before Abraham Lincoln's assassination, the President signed Bonneville's promotion to Brigadier General.

On June 12, 1878, Benjamin Bonneville died. Yet through Washington Irving's pen, Bonneville's fame has lived on.

Today, as we drive past the tributes our modern world offers to his memory, we ought to take a moment to recall the man, an American patriot.

Bonneville Point

Take the Blacks Creek/Kuna Road Exit 64 off I-84, 9.8 miles east of Boise. Drive north on Blacks Creek Road 2.4 miles and turn left at the green state historical sign. Bonneville Point is 1.4 miles beyond.

GENERAL B. L. E. BONNEVILLE

General B.L.E. Bonneville: An American patriot. Courtesy of Denver Public Library.

A reenactment of fording the Snake River at Three Island Crossing State Park in Glenns Ferry, Idaho.

NARCISSA WHITMAN

In July 1836 at the Green River Rendezvous held near today's Pinedale, Wyoming, the trappers considered Dr. Marcus Whitman the luckiest man alive. For hours on end they paraded past his camp as though they were preened peacocks. Every mountain man in the promenade had donned his finest buckskin shirt and fringed leggings, and each one of them craned his neck, seeking a glimpse of the doctor's radiant wife.

The blond Narcissa Whitman was as lovely as she was vivacious. No man could resist her disarming smile or sparkling blue eyes, which absorbed everything with unbounded enthusiasm in this alien world of fur trappers and feathered warriors.

Narcissa had come to the rendezvous en route to the mission she and her husband planned establishing among the Cayuse Indians in eastern Oregon. She and Marcus had begun their journey two weeks after their February wedding in Angelica, New York. At Cincinnati the newlyweds were joined by Henry Spalding and his wife, Eliza, who intended opening a mission for the Nez Perce.

Sailing aboard steamboats, the Whitmans and Spaldings descended the Ohio River and then churned up the Mississippi to St. Louis. From there they steamed up the Missouri River toward Independence. As the missionaries hurried to reach the American Fur Company's supply caravan before it began its trek to the mountain men's summer rendezvous, they rounded out their party with a missionary-mechanic named William Gray, two roustabout adventurers, and three Indian boys.

In May the missionaries turned their backs to the settlements and caught up to the fur company's pack caravan on the Platte River in eastern Nebraska. Much of the time Narcissa rode sidesaddle, but the uneven jostling proved too painful for Eliza, who preferred the relative comfort of a wagon.

In June the women visited Fort Lucien on eastern Wyoming's Laramie River (although the trading post was often referred to as Fort Laramie, it wasn't officially named that until the U.S. Army bought it in 1849). On the Fourth of July they became the first white women to cross the Continental Divide at Wyoming's South Pass.

Two days later they arrived at the Green River Rendezvous, and every mountain man who had ever skinned a beaver immediately fell in love with Narcissa. The dour Eliza Spalding excited as much attention as a Saturday night bath.

When the rendezvous ended, the missionaries continued their trip under the protection of a Hudson's Bay Company brigade led by John McLeod and Tom McKay. Although the Hudson's Bay men were courteous to Eliza, it was Narcissa who captured their hearts.

On August 3 the party reached Fort Hall on the Snake River, making Narcissa and Eliza the first white women to set foot in Idaho. Joseph Thing, the trading post's *bourgeois* (commander), opened the fort to the missionaries and supplemented their all-meat diet with fresh vegetables and bread. As she had done with McLeod and McKay, Narcissa enchanted the *bourgeois* with her charms.

From Fort Hall the Hudson's Bay brigade and missionaries headed west along the south side of the Snake River. The two commanders did what they could to ease the hardships of travel, but they could do nothing to stem the August heat and incessant mosquitoes. Each day the sun etched the squint lines at the corners of Narcissa's eyes a wee bit deeper.

At Two Island Crossing downstream from today's Glenns Ferry, the party forded to the north bank of the Snake River. Riding tall horses, Narcissa and Eliza braved the five-foot-deep water, proving their mettle and showing that women could handle the rigors of what would soon become the Oregon Trail.

On August 19 they reached Fort Boise near the mouth of the Boise River. Tom McKay, who had built the post two years before, gave Narcissa and Eliza every luxury the trading post had to offer, but what the women relished most was the opportunity to wash their clothes. It marked the third time in three and a half months that they could do laundry.

Three days later Narcissa and Eliza again forded the Snake River on horseback, leaving Idaho and riding toward Fort Wall Walla and their life's work. Eliza Spalding and her husband returned to Idaho in late November, establishing their Nez Perce mission in the Lapwai Valley, two miles from the Clearwater River.

The Whitmans founded their mission at Waiilatpu on the Walla Walla River in today's southeastern Washington, about 25 miles upstream from the Hudson's Bay Company's Fort Walla Walla (at the time this country was part of the Oregon Territory). Three months after moving into her new home, Narcissa celebrated turning 29 years old by giving birth to a daughter.

During the next 10 years Dr. Marcus Whitman ministered to the spiritual and physical needs of the Cayuse Indians, while his beautiful wife aged before her time. America's great westward migration brought streams of Oregon-bound immigrants seeking food and care for their sick at the Waiilatpu Mission. Narcissa shared the fruits of her garden, and Marcus tended broken bones and applied poultices.

Although the Whitmans' kindness was a godsend to the weary travelers, it was a curse to the Indians, for in 1847 the immigrants arrived with measles. The infected white children fretted a week or two with mild fevers and rashes before getting well, but in that time the disease passed to the Cayuse. The virus raced through the tribe, killing Indian sons and daughters by the score.

When the epidemic finally exhausted its reservoir of human fuel, half of the tribe lay dead, and the survivors were lusting for vengeance. As the Indians cast about for the cause of their affliction, their rancor turned toward the Whitmans.

On November 29 the Cayuses took their revenge, murdering 14 people at the Waiilatpu Mission. Among the victims were Marcus Whitman and his graying wife, Narcissa.

SIGHTS TO SEE

Three Island Crossing State Park

From I-84 Exits 120 or 121 drive into Glenns Ferry and turn south on Commercial Street, which swings west near the river where the street name changes to Madison. The park is two miles ahead.

Each August reenactors float across the Snake River at Three Island Crossing State Park via a 19-century ferry. Afterwards other reenactors ford the waterway in covered wagons, which are accompanied by outriders and members of the Paiute-Shoshone tribe.

Oregon Trail immigrants forded the Snake River at two points near Glenns Ferry. Three Island Crossing at the state park was the easier of the two. Narcissa Whitman and Eliza Spalding forded one mile upstream at Two Island Crossing.

Henry and Eliza Spaldings' Mission

Located in the Nez Perce National Historical Park off US 95 north of Lapwai (east of Lewiston).

Narcissa Whitman. Courtesy of NPS

BEN HUDSPETH'S
Idaho Shortcut

In mid-July 1849 a large wagon train with 250 emigrants left the Oregon Trail at Sheep Rock, not far from modern-day Soda Springs, Idaho. The train's leaders, Benoni Morgan Hudspeth and John J. Myers hoped to shave a week off their trip to the California goldfields by heading due west, thereby avoiding the longer route via Fort Hall. During the subsequent years of America's great westering, thousands of pioneers used this detour, which was called Hudspeth's Cutoff.

Ben Hudspeth had grown up in Missouri, 11 miles from Independence. In the 1830s he watched heavy freight wagons lumber past his family's farm as their teamsters began the arduous journey along the Santa Fe Trail to New Mexico. Hudspeth also saw mule trains packing supplies to the fur trappers' mountain rendezvous and then returning some months later with their loads of beaver pelts. In time this northern trappers' route became the Oregon Trail.

In the spring of 1845 Hudspeth joined John Frémont's topographical expedition to map the upper Arkansas River. Among the party's more notable members were Joe Walker and Kit Carson, former fur trappers who had forged their well-earned reputations in the wilds of the Rocky Mountains. After leaving part of his force at Bent's Fort (in eastern Colorado) so the men could complete the Arkansas River survey, the politically-connected Frémont and the remainder of his party crossed the Continental Divide and Great Basin before heading into California. Among those going with him were Carson, Walker, and Hudspeth.

In 1846 the United States went to war with Mexico, and Frémont seized the opportunity to foment California's Bear Flag Revolt. Ben Hudspeth served as an officer in Frémont's California Battalion until 1847 when its commander was censored by the U.S. Government for exceeding his orders. That summer Hudspeth returned to Missouri, but the lure of California remained in his blood.

After gold was discovered near Sutter's sawmill at the western foot of the Sierra Nevada Mountains, Ben Hudspeth persuaded four of his brothers to join him in a trading venture to the diggings. John Myers was recruited as the party's pilot. Myers was a former mountain man who had also been with Frémont's California expedition. Rounding out the party were emigrants willing to pay to be guided to the new El Dorado. All together the train numbered about 40 wagons.

The Hudspeth brothers' cargo consisted of not only shovels, picks, and gold pans—the tools needed in order to harvest wealth from the gold-rich placers—but also playing cards and liquor, goods likely to be in high demand in the rough California mining camps. Wanting to see his sons well mounted, William Hudspeth, Ben's father, gave each of them a fine thoroughbred.

On May 1, 1849, the Hudspeth wagon train rolled away from Independence. Counting oxen, mules, saddlehorses, and beef cattle, the train's stock totaled 600 head. Because of the experience of Ben Hudspeth and John Myers, the party reached the Bear River without difficulty. During their time with Frémont, the two guides had learned of a trace that ran west from the Bear and threaded its way through four mountain ranges before connecting with the main trail to California. For those going to the goldfields speed was paramount to all other considerations. Hudspeth and Myers knew if they could follow the old trace and find water and grass for their animals, they would gain time on parties that had started ahead of them.

On Thursday, July 19, they turned off the primary trail and rolled west toward the Portneuf Range, where they discovered a hot springs, which later travelers dubbed Dempsey's Bath Tub (today, Idaho's Lava Hot Springs). From there they wound through the Bannock Range, crossed the Arbon Valley, and dipped below the Deep Creek Mountains to Twin Springs. Their route picked its way over the Sublett Range (Idaho's Sublett Range is spelled without the ending "e" that Bill Sublette used in his last name), and then pushed almost due west to the Raft River and the California

The defeat of Bear Hunter broke the Shoshones' will to fight. In early July Chief Washakie negotiated a peace treaty on behalf of the Eastern Shoshones. Then two weeks later Pocatello sent word to the American authorities that he, too, wished a truce.

On July 30, 1863, Pocatello and eight other Northwestern Shoshone chiefs signed the Treaty of Box Elder (in Utah) with Connor and Indian Superintendent James Doty. In exchange for peace Pocatello's people forfeited over two-thirds of their homeland. Henceforth, they would be restricted to the country lying between the Raft River and Portneuf Mountains. In addition, the Indians agreed to permit free passage through their territory by wagon trains, telegraph crews, stagecoaches, and the railroad. In return the U.S. Government promised the Shoshones a meager $5,000 per year in food and blankets.

Over the next three months Superintendent Doty secured similar treaties with the Western Shoshones, Gosiutes, and several small hybrid bands living near the Bear River.

From the start the annuities were never sufficient to care for all the Indians. That the supplies were invariably late and always short merely made a bad situation intolerable. Unwilling to sit by and watch his people starve, Pocatello began looting food from the stagecoach relay stations that Ben Holladay was stringing across northern Utah and southeastern Idaho. When Holladay complained to the Army, Patrick Connor—now General Connor—threw Pocatello in jail, vowing to rid himself of the troublesome chief, once and for all. However, after the Superintendent cautioned Connor there would be a full-blown Indian war if Pocatello were hanged, the general turned the chief loose.

Over the years, the Mormons had always been far more sympathetic to the Shoshones' plight than had either the U.S. Army or non-Mormons. After the tribal elders signed the peace treaties, the inadequate government rations compelled their people to beg at Mormon farms. When the Latter Day Saints gave the Indians food, gentile settlers in southeastern Idaho and northern Utah viewed the kindness with suspicion, fearing the Mormons would induce the Shoshones to pillage non-Mormon homesteads. Gentile newspapers inflamed the racial and religious prejudice of their readers by printing false stories about Indian atrocities.

After the Fort Hall Reservation opened in the late 1860s Indian agents pressed the Shoshones and Bannocks to give up their traditional homeland and settle there. During the next several years the scattered Indian bands, including Pocatello's, drifted onto the reservation, lured by the government's promise of increased rations. Of course the annuities weren't sufficient to feed all the people that the soldiers crowded onto the reservation. As a result the Indians continued begging at nearby Mormon farms.

Eager for the larger handouts that went to those who embraced the LDS religion, Pocatello went to Salt Lake City in May 1875, where he was baptized and ordained a church elder.

During this time the government moved Shoshones from Wyoming's Wind River Mountains and Idaho's Lemhi country onto the Fort Hall Reservation, further stretching the meager annuities. Driven by hunger, other Indians followed in Pocatello's footsteps and headed to Utah to be baptized. By the end of July the number of Native American LDS proselytes approached 600.

Alarmed by this growing exodus to the Mormon enclaves, northern Utah gentiles petitioned the Army at Camp Douglas to force the Indians back on the reservation. The post commander warned the Shoshones he would send out the cavalry unless they returned to Idaho. Fearing another slaughter, Pocatello and the other converts submitted and fled to Fort Hall.

Now in his 60s, Pocatello kept to the country near Bannock Creek, avoiding the agency headquarters and the political wrangling which occupied the other chiefs. During the Bannock War of 1878 he stayed on the reservation and didn't fight. His last official appearance occurred on November 14, 1881, when he added his name alongside the other tribal leaders who agreed to sell part of the Fort Hall Reservation.

Over the following three years Pocatello's health deteriorated. By October 1884 he knew the end was at hand. At his behest, his family and friends took him to the Snake River above the American Falls. He passed away a few days later. As he had requested, his wives tied his guns, knives, and other possessions to his body, and several of the young men buried him in a large, aquifer-fed spring. In tribute to his memory, the Indians killed 18 of Pocatello's ponies and sank them atop his watery grave.

Today Pocatello's resting place lies beneath the American Falls Reservoir.

Pioneer inscriptions written in axle grease at the City of Rocks National Reserve.

City of Rocks National Reserve

From I-84 Exit 216 (between Burley and the I-84/I-86 interchange) drive south on Idaho State Road 77 approximately 21 miles. Turn west (right) on the Elba-Almo Road and drive another 17 miles to Almo. From the National Park Service office in Almo, continue south 0.7 mile and turn west (right) on the City of Rocks Road. The Reserve entrance is 1.6 miles ahead.

The first known white men to see the City of Rocks were members of a Hudson's Bay Company fur trapping brigade led by Peter Skene Ogden in 1826. With the start of the California gold rush in 1849, the number of annual visitors to the area jumped precipitously, with 52,000 emigrants camping there in 1852 alone.

Many travelers on the California Trail wrote their names with axle grease on the Reserve's granite boulders. Some of the signatures are still visible.

Today the City of Rocks is one of the premier rock climbing areas in the United States, offering hundreds of technical climbing routes on monoliths such as the Bread Loaves, Bath Rock, and Incisor. "Hard men" and beginners alike will find ample challenge.

For those who prefer keeping their feet on the ground, the City has numerous hiking trails. Each spring and early summer, wildflowers transform the meadows into colorful mosaics, while in the fall yellow-leafed aspens paint the hillsides with brilliant hues.

The Reserve is home to deer, elk, coyotes, and porcupines. Birds include golden eagles, hawks, doves, and vultures. **Beware, there are also rattlesnakes.**

If your interest lies in history, rock climbing, hiking, or merely visiting beautiful places, the City of Rocks has something for everyone.

City of Rocks National Reserve

From I-84 Exit 216 (between Burley and the I-84/I-86 interchange) drive south on Idaho State Road 77 approximately 21 miles. Turn west (right) on the Elba-Almo Road and drive another 17 miles to Almo. From the National Park Service office in Almo, continue south 0.7 mile and turn west (right) on the City of Rocks Road. The Reserve entrance is 1.6 miles ahead.

The first known white men to see the City of Rocks were members of a Hudson's Bay Company fur trapping brigade led by Peter Skene Ogden in 1826. With the start of the California gold rush in 1849, the number of annual visitors to the area jumped precipitously, with 52,000 emigrants camping there in 1852 alone.

Many travelers on the California Trail wrote their names with axle grease on the Reserve's granite boulders. Some of the signatures are still visible.

Today the City of Rocks is one of the premier rock climbing areas in the United States, offering hundreds of technical climbing routes on monoliths such as the Bread Loaves, Bath Rock, and Incisor. "Hard men" and beginners alike will find ample challenge.

For those who prefer keeping their feet on the ground, the City has numerous hiking trails. Each spring and early summer, wildflowers transform the meadows into colorful mosaics, while in the fall yellow-leafed aspens paint the hillsides with brilliant hues.

The Reserve is home to deer, elk, coyotes, and porcupines. Birds include golden eagles, hawks, doves, and vultures. **Beware, there are also rattlesnakes.**

If your interest lies in history, rock climbing, hiking, or merely visiting beautiful places, the City of Rocks has something for everyone.

POCATELLO

Standing at the Crossroads

Pocatello, Idaho, traces its roots to northern Utah, where the Northwestern Shoshone chief *Tonaioza* signed the Treaty of Box Elder on July 30, 1863. Of course, General Patrick Connor, who had conducted the bloody campaign that induced *Tonaioza's* surrender, knew the chief by the name used by the area's white settlers: Pocatello.

The Box Elder peace treaty chopped off vast portions of the Northwestern Shoshones' territory, but more devastating, it granted an easement over the tribe's remaining land. Safe passage was now guaranteed for the families and miners rushing to Oregon, California, and the Montana goldfields.

The New York "Stagecoach King," Ben Holladay, soon opened a stage line along the Montana Trail, which ran from the Mormon settlements north of Salt Lake City, past old Fort Hall, to the diggings west of Helena. Spaced every 12 to 15 miles along the route were swing stations, where the exhausted horses could be exchanged for fresh. Home stations were set farther apart and provided travelers a place to rest and grab a meal.

Along the Portneuf River, swing stations were located at Robbers Roost Creek, Black Rock Canyon, and a stream that was named for Chief *Tonaioza*: Pocatello Creek.

In the late 1860s the government opened the Fort Hall Indian Reservation and began pressuring bands of Shoshones and Bannocks to move within its confines, which encompassed Pocatello Station.

In 1874 the Utah Northern Railroad was completed from Logan, Utah, to Franklin, Idaho. Freight bound for the four thousand gold and silver mines of western Montana had to be off-loaded at the railhead in Franklin, then hauled north in mule-drawn wagons. Returning wagons carried ore—three million pounds per year. Except in the most inclement weather, six to seven dozen wagons a day lumbered past Pocatello Station and the other southeastern Idaho stage stops.

In 1877 Jay Gould, the New York financier who controlled the Union Pacific Railway, bought the Utah Northern, reorganized it as the Utah and Northern Railroad Company, and sold it to the Union Pacific's other shareholders. Although the Utah and Northern was legally separate from the Union Pacific, its owners considered it to be an adjunct.

Eager to milk the lucrative Montana freight market, Gould set crews to laying track from Franklin up the Marsh Creek Valley to the Portneuf River, past Pocatello Station to Eagle Rock (the future Idaho Falls), then north over the Continental Divide to Butte and Garrison, Montana, where the rails connected with the Northern Pacific line.

Needing to make its trespass of the Fort Hall Indian Reservation legal, the Utah and Northern officials paid the Shoshone and Bannock tribes for the right-of-way and bought 40 acres around Pocatello Station. Because the Pocatello site was surrounded by Indian land, the railroad constructed its maintenance facilities at Eagle Rock.

The Utah and Northern soon began earning a substantial profit. In 1885 the year after the railway was completed, Montana ore shipments increased over 80 fold to 250 million pounds.

Meanwhile, during the time the Utah and Northern was being built, Union Pacific officials sought to extend their tracks to the West Coast, thereby making their system transcontinental. In 1880 east-bound freight from the Willamette and Columbia River valleys had to be shipped south to San Francisco, then carried east on Central Pacific trains to Utah, where it finally joined the Union Pacific line. Wanting to tap Oregon's rapid growth as well as prevent competitors such as the Northern Pacific from cutting the Union Pacific off from the coastal markets, the U.P. directors decided to build their own branch to Portland. Because the tangled U.S. transportation laws prevented the Union Pacific from owning the span directly, its stockholders formed another quasi-subsidiary: The Oregon Short Line Railroad.

In 1881 construction gangs started laying track from the

Union Pacific's main line in Granger, Wyoming. The following year the rails crossed those of the Utah and Northern at Pocatello Station. The lower Snake River was bridged in 1884, and in November that year, the Oregon Short Line opened for commerce along its entire length.

With the completion of the Utah and Northern and Oregon Short Line, the crossroads at Pocatello Station gained importance. In 1887 the Shoshone and Bannock tribes sold another 1,840 acres around the junction, prompting the Union Pacific to shift its maintenance operations from Eagle Rock to Pocatello. Almost overnight, Pocatello became a boomtown as stores, saloons, and other enterprises sprang up to support the railroad employees. However, because the Fort Hall Indian Reservation still surrounded the village, there was a limit to Pocatello's growth.

About this time, Congress passed the Dawes Severalty Act in an effort to reduce the dependence of Native Americans on federal assistance. Across the West, Indian families were coerced onto 160-acre farms, leaving vast, "excess" portions of their reservations available to be sold to the government. This unneeded land was then given to white homesteaders.

In 1898 the Shoshone and Bannock tribes offered to sell 654 square miles of the Fort Hall Reservation's south end for $1.44 per acre. Two years later Congress approved the trade and title passed to the government. Pocatello was no longer a landlocked island.

In late spring 1902, people from far and wide collected in Pocatello as federal officials prepared to open the former reservation to homesteading. Although 40-acre plots near town were sold at auction, most everyone came for the land rush, which would allow a man or woman to get a free farm.

At noon on June 17 hundreds of would-be Idahoans raced onto the prairie south of Pocatello to stake their claims and then dashed to file them at the land office in Blackfoot. When the dust finally settled, Pocatello was well on its way to becoming one of Idaho's premier cities.

Today ribbons of asphalt vie with the railroads for passengers and freight. Yet the junction of I-15 and I-86 ensures that Pocatello will remain a city at the crossroads.

Bannock County Museum

In south Pocatello take I-15 Exit 67, turning right on 5th Ave. north. In 0.6 mile turn left on Fredregill Rd., then go left again on 4th Ave. south. In 0.3 mile turn right at the sign for Upper Ross Park. The museum sits at the top of the hill.

Among the museum's many exhibits is a Concord mud wagon that once belonged to Ben Holladay's stagecoach company. Mud wagons were lightweight passenger coaches, capable of traveling the steep, often muddy roads of the inter-mountain west. Unlike the heavier and more costly Concord stagecoaches of the day, mud wagons had a boxy, rawboned appearance.

One of the museum's most striking displays is a mural wall depicting Pocatello's history. The reliefs were sandblasted into polished marble and then painted by Tim Norton.

Lower Ross Park

From the Bannock County Museum, return to Fredregill Rd. and drive 0.3 mile to 2nd St. Turn left and continue 0.3 mile to a large parking lot on the right. A railroad display is behind the swimming pool complex. Train buffs will enjoy seeing the 1900-vintage Oregon Short Line caboose, a 1911 Mikado steam locomotive, and a 1960s-vintage Centennial Series diesel.

According to Pocatello resident Fred Dykes, who spent many hours restoring these pieces, the steam locomotive received the "Mikado" name because Japan was the first country to buy this type of engine. During World War II the Union Pacific renamed the model "MacArthur."

JOHN MULLAN'S ROAD

On July 4, 1861, a young Army officer stood in the dense forest of Idaho's panhandle, watching one of his soldiers burn the date and the initials "M.R." into a tall pine tree. During the past two years, Captain John Mullan had seen M.R. emblazoned 624 times, once for every mile of his Mullan Road.

Of course the War Department never intended the road be named for its builder. The initials meant Military Road. But in truth, though the Army was paying its $230,000-cost, the road really belonged to the single-minded determination of John Mullan.

The genesis of Mullan's road began 15 years earlier. On June 15, 1846, the United States and Great Britain settled the western U.S.-Canadian boundary along the 49th parallel. The compromise agreement brought the Oregon Territory—now the states of Oregon, Washington, and Idaho, plus sizeable pieces of western Wyoming and Montana—into the American fold. Although the two countries had jointly occupied this vast land for 28 years, from the mid-1830s onward a floodtide of American emigrants crossing the Oregon Trail tilted the country for the United States.

In the years that followed the border settlement, increasing numbers of Americans continued flocking to the Oregon Territory, eventually straining the resources of its territorial government. In 1853 Congress carved the Washington Territory—made up of Washington, northern Idaho, and western Montana—from the Oregon Territory, appointing General Isaac Stevens as its governor. In addition to his other duties, Stevens was given responsibility for choosing a railroad route across the northern Continental Divide. The lawmakers had already determined the necessity of a rail line running from St. Paul, Minnesota, to the growing population center around Puget Sound, Washington.

The following year General Stevens assigned the route-picking job to Lieutenant John Mullan, who had graduated from West

Point as a topographical engineer two years before. Mullan's orders were to survey a wagon road from Fort Walla Walla, the old Hudson's Bay Company trading post on the Columbia River (near Wallula, Washington) to Fort Benton, Pierre Chouteau Jr. & Company's westernmost trading post on the Missouri River (now Fort Benton, Montana). Congress figured the wagon road could serve as a northern alternative to the Oregon Trail until such time as a rail line could be laid over the roadbed.

Funded by a Congressional appropriation of $30,000, Lieutenant Mullan crisscrossed the Bitterroot Mountains six times, logging over 1,000 miles through some of the harshest terrain in the United States, as he reconnoitered a suitable route. After receiving his recommendation, Army paper shufflers filed it away, deeming other projects to be of higher priority.

In 1858 Native Americans in the Pacific Northwest grew resentful of the white emigrants who were stealing their land. Wanting to regain their tribal birthright, the Indians went on the warpath. Although the Army soon quelled the unrest (Lieutenant Mullan commanded Nez Perce scouts during the fighting), the hostilities persuaded Congress that the nation urgently needed a military road linking the region's two major waterways.

On the Columbia River shallow-draft steamboats could travel to Wallula, Washington. The Hudson's Bay Company had abandoned its nearby Fort Walla Walla trading post in the fall of 1855 because of Indian unrest, and the following year, the Army had constructed a military fortification of the same name (where the city of Walla Walla, Washington now sits) about 30 miles east of the Wallula landing.

On the Missouri River steamboat pilots were continually pushing the envelope of westward navigation, each year coming ever closer to Fort Benton. Most people assumed it was merely a matter of time before a steamer made it all the way to the trading post. When that occurred, all that would be needed for the lower Columbia River Valley and upper Missouri to be connected would be for someone to build a road over the Bitterroot Mountains.

Resurrecting John Mullan's dusty report, the Army secured $230,000 in Congressional funding and in the summer of 1859, ordered the lieutenant to begin work.

Late that June Mullan assembled 100 enlisted men, two junior officers, and 100 civilians at the Army's Fort Walla Walla (a road already connected the Army garrison with the Wallula Landing on the Columbia River) and started construction. As the crews added each new mile to the route, a workman erected a marker emblazoned with the mileage to that point and the initials M.R. for Military Road.

Within a month Mullan's road-building brigade had crossed the Columbia Plateau (in eastern Washington) and reached the wetlands south of Idaho's Coeur d'Alene Lake. Progress now slowed to a crawl as crews erected a 60-foot bridge over the marshes, established a ferry across the St. Joe River, and chopped countless trees to lay a corduroy passageway atop the boggy terrain. On August 18, 1859, Mullan's road passed the Coeur d'Alene Mission of the Sacred Heart (known today as the Cataldo Mission of the Sacred Heart, it is the oldest building in Idaho), where the mileage marker read "M.R. 199 Miles."

Meanwhile, the Coeur d'Alene Indians became alarmed about having a white man's road cutting through their land. Hearing that a number of chiefs were urging their warriors to attack his crews, Mullan cautioned the tribal leaders he would hang any Indian who interfered with his work. Taking the lieutenant at his word, the Coeur d'Alenes backed down.

From the Sacred Heart Mission the construction brigade pushed east along the Coeur d'Alene River. Now in some of the densest timber in North America, the crews battled with axes and saws for every yard of progress. Day after day Mullan's road grew from muscle and sweat as the men hacked a swath through trees that grew as thick as grass.

Where the hillsides were steep, the crews dug their roadbed into the slopes. When mountain streams blocked the path, carpenters spanned the frothing water with bridges, erecting so many that history has lost count of their number. Determined that nothing would hinder his progress, Lieutenant Mullan squelched a rumor of gold when one of his workmen discovered placer deposits along the North Fork of the Coeur d'Alene River.

Week after week the brutal work continued, until at last, John Mullan ran head-on against a force his willpower could not overcome—winter. Heavy snowfall forced everyone into camp. Chafing at the inactivity, the lieutenant counted the days until spring. His lone satisfaction came in knowing that his road had crested the Bitterroot Mountains. The heavy growth on the eastern slope of the range still needed to be penetrated, but at least he had reached Montana.

In February 1860 Mullan decided that winter had delayed him long enough. With snow still holding up work in the Bitterroots, he leapfrogged part of his brigade to the Clark Fork River, where crews established a ferry and began building their road upstream along the right bank. The men still camping in the Bitterroots had to wait until late March before the snow melted sufficiently for them to start chopping and shoveling their way down from the mountains. Because the country was so rugged, it took them until the end of June to link their portion of the road to the Clark Fork Ferry.

Following the Clark Fork River Valley, the work steadily progressed until a six-mile-long bluff forced Mullan to veer away from the bottomland. It took 150 men a month and a half to skirt the obstruction.

From here the terrain eased, allowing a rapid push past the future town site of Missoula and on up the valley carved by the Clark Fork. At the mouth of the Little Blackfoot River, Mullan turned east, following the tributary until he could swing north toward a gentle, 5,902-foot pass that now bears his name.

On July 17 Lieutenant Mullan's road crested the Continental Divide just west of Helena, Montana. After coming down from the mountains, the crews headed north to Little Prickly Pear Creek. Eventually the stream's narrow canyon threatened to choke off the route, compelling Mullan to construct his road over Medicine Rock Mountain. Upon reaching Wolf Creek, the workmen pushed due north to the Dearborn River and then veered northeast toward easier country.

Section of original Mullan Road in the Fourth of July Canyon.

With the end now so near, the pace became frantic. The crews almost leapt across the plains of the upper Missouri, passing Lionhead and Birdtail Buttes, fording the Sun River, edging around Twenty-Eight-Mile Spring, and then racing for the Missouri. On August 1, 1860, a day after John Mullan's 30th birthday, a workman branded the 624-mile marker at Fort Benton.

A month earlier, as Mullan's crews were still crawling up the west side of the Continental Divide, the steamboats *Chippewa* and *Key West No. 2* had made the first steamed passage to the upper Missouri trading post. Among the boats' passengers were 300 soldiers, who had orders to march to Fort Walla Walla via the new Military Road. The soldiers began their journey shortly after the road builders reached the Missouri River. It took the troopers 57 days to traverse what Mullan's crews had spent a year building.

The amount of labor expended by Mullan's workmen is nearly beyond belief. Along a 120-mile section of the route—most of them in the Bitterroot Mountains—they had sawed and chopped a 25-foot-wide lane through dense forest. If placed end to end, the collective road cuts would exceed 30 miles, all of them dug by hand. And every river and stream the route crossed was spanned with a bridge or ferry.

John Mullan may have completed his original mission, but his work was far from finished. During the late winter and early spring of 1860, while he was still pushing his route through the Clark Fork River Valley, he received reports that flooding south of Coeur d'Alene Lake had made that section of his road unusable. It needed to be moved to the high ground north of the lake.

In early 1861 Congress approved $100,000 in additional funds to allow portions of the road to be rerouted. Promoted to captain, John Mullan began repairing and altering his original track. In the spring of that year, he relocated the road north of Coeur d'Alene Lake. He then bored east through thick timber, planning to link up to his original road at the Sacred Heart Mission.

On July 4 in the heavily wooded Coeur d'Alene Mountains, about six miles east of Coeur d'Alene Lake, Captain Mullan gave his crews the day off to celebrate the nation's birthday. While most of his men cheered Old Glory and the Union, one of their number branded the date and the initials M.R. on a stately white pine that bordered their route. Captain Mullan must have smiled when he looked at the blaze, knowing that although M.R. meant Military Road, a few people were already calling it the Mullan Road.

Mullan needed until August to tie his new route into the old one at the Sacred Heart Mission. From here his crews continued up the Coeur d'Alene River, improving the original road. Winter again caught them in the mountains, forcing them onto a starvation diet and compelling them to eat their horses.

By now the Civil War was consuming the government's resources, siphoning off funds that should have been earmarked for the roadway's maintenance. Spring flooding in 1862 wrecked many stretches of the Mullan Road, but Congress failed to appropriate any money for repairs.

Because the Mullan Road never received the military traffic that John Mullan had envisioned, he published a guide in 1865, attempting to spur civilian use. His efforts were only partly successful. By 1866 an estimated 20,000 people had traveled some portion of the route, most of them going back and forth from the Montana goldfields (in the mountains around Helena) to Fort Benton. Some of the more unusual parties to use the road were camel packers, who supplied the gold miners via camel caravans.

With the government refusing to provide funds for road maintenance—even after the Civil War ended—traffic declined. A few cattlemen herded livestock along usable portions of the route in the 1870s and '80s, but by and large, the Mullan Road fell into disrepair.

As a final insult to John Mullan's labor, the owners of the Northern Pacific Railway declined to use the road for a right-of-way across the Continental Divide. Instead the railroad men opted to lay their tracks well north of Mullan's route, choosing to go past Idaho's Lake Pend Oreille.

When John Mullan died in 1909, the forest had already reclaimed most of his work. But time has confirmed the wisdom of his route. Today across Idaho's panhandle and into western Montana, Interstate 90 follows much of the Mullan Road.

Mullan Tree Historical Site

Readers wishing to see a section of the Mullan Road may do so in the Fourth of July Canyon, 13 miles east of Coeur d'Alene. To reach the historical site, drive I-90 through Idaho's panhandle, turning off at Exit 28. From the state historical sign, follow a paved road a short way downhill to a statue of John Mullan. From the parking area, a ½-mile nature trail follows a remnant of the Mullan Road. As you walk the trail, you'll pass a stone monument that used to mark the pine tree that Mullan's workman carved on July 4, 1861.

In 1962 a windstorm broke off the top of the Mullan Tree, as the historic pine has come to be known. At the time it was estimated to be nearly 325 years old. In 1988 the tree's blazed stump was removed to the Museum of North Idaho, where it is now on display. The museum is located at 115 North West Boulevard, Coeur d'Alene, ID 83816.

John Mullan Memorial in the Fourth of July Canyon.

THE BEAR RIVER
Massacre

The young soldiers in Colonel Patrick Connor's California Volunteers shivered in their saddles as dawn slowly erased the shadows off the Bear River's icy banks. To the north smoke from the clustered tepees heralded that the Shoshones hadn't run. The greenest blue-clad recruit knew the Indians would fight.

Across the river from the troopers, a lone brave reined in his steaming pony. For the past quarter hour the warrior had raced to and fro, taunting the soldiers to attack. Now as his mount pawed the frozen ground for a tuft of grass, the Shoshone sat in silence. Among the Volunteers, the crisp air amplified the sounds of waiting: the squeak of leather, sloshing canteens, the neighs of nervous horses, muffled coughs.

"Major McGarry!"

"Sir?"

"Move 'em out!"

At the Colonel's command, the soldiers plunged their horses into the frigid stream. The animals balked at the cold until the cavalrymen raked their flanks with spurs.

After coming out of the water, the Major formed his troop into fours-abreast. A moment later, the bugler signaled "charge," propelling the rank toward a ravine where Chief Bear Hunter and 300 warriors lay hidden.

Before leaving California, Colonel Connor had petitioned Army headquarters, asking to take his soldiers east to fight the Confederates. Instead of granting the request and allowing Connor to win glory in the Civil War, the brass sent him to Utah to monitor the Mormons. In October 1862 the disgruntled commander erected Camp Douglas near the LDS enclaves east of the Great Salt Lake.

When Shoshones killed a white miner near Franklin in present-day Idaho, Connor opted to vent his ire on Indians in lieu of southern rebels. Despite sub-zero temperatures, the Colonel marched his troops up Cache Valley, reaching the Bear River village in late afternoon, January 28, 1863.

Just after sunrise the next morning, Connor launched the bloodiest Indian massacre in the history of the United States.

Bear Hunter's warriors met the cavalry charge with a withering barrage of arrows and lead. Fourteen soldiers tumbled dead on the snowy plain before Major McGarry ordered his troopers to fight on foot.

As soon as the infantry forded the river and joined the cavalry's line, Colonel Connor sent part of his force to enfilade the Indian stronghold. Within minutes the Shoshones were caught in a lethal cross fire. Outgunned, those still alive bolted for their village, hoping to save their families.

With "Take no prisoners!" echoing in their ears, the California Volunteers descended on the fleeing tribe. When the soldiers finished their slaughter, the snowy ground coursed red with blood. The hacked and punctured bodies of Indian men, women, and children littered the landscape as if they were human cordwood scattered by a vengeful whirlwind.

Counting those who later died from their wounds, Colonel Connor lost 22 men, most in the initial assault. The families of Franklin cared for the injured soldiers until they could return to Camp Douglas. But before reaching the warmth of the Mormon homes, 79 troopers saw their fingers and toes blackened by frostbite.

The Shoshones mourned 368 dead, including Chief Bear Hunter. Only a handful of warriors escaped. Among the women and children, the soldiers spared only 164.

Over 2½ times more Indians were killed in this southeastern Idaho battle than fell at either Sand Creek or Wounded Knee.

In the aftermath of the carnage, the Army pinned a "victory" star to Patrick Connor's collar, promoting him to Brigadier General. The Shoshones received a far more dubious reward. Disheartened by the defeat, the surviving bands made peace with the U.S. Government. Then in a series of treaties, a broken people signed away its tribal birthright.

The Bear River Massacre Monument (erected by the Daughters of Utah Pioneers and now a National Historic Landmark)

Located three miles north of Preston on US 91. The turn-out is one-half mile north of the Bear River bridge.

Much of the actual battle site is on private land. In order to see it, drive 50 yards north of the memorial, turning west on Hot Springs Road. In 0.1 mile go right on 1500 W; after 0.2 mile cross an irrigation ditch and park at the gate.

Most of the slaughter took place below in Battle Creek Ravine (unfortunately, now used as a dump). The massacre site can also be seen from the west side of US 91 just as it starts up the grade about 0.2 mile north of the monument.

Bear River Crossing on a cold January day, looking much as it did over a century ago when Patrick Connor's California Volunteers launched the bloodiest Indian massacre in the history of the United States.

Wilson Butte Cave on the Snake River Plain, where prehistoric man once hunted camels.

WHEN THE CAMELS
Returned to Idaho

Tom McNear sighted his rifle just behind his target's left shoulder. Holding his breath, the greenhorn hunter slowly squeezed the slack from his trigger. The excitement of finding a half dozen moose clustered so close together made his heart race. It was nearly impossible for him to hold his aim.

When he fired, the black powder smoke billowed before his eyes. For a moment he feared the noise of his shot had scattered the herd. As he reloaded, he nervously glanced toward his fallen prey. Seeing that the remaining herd had strayed but a few steps, McNear could hardly control his glee. Again pulling the rifle stock to his shoulder, he settled on his next prize, this time leveling his sights slightly below the animal's prominent hump.

"*Arrêtez! Arrêtez!* Are you crazy?" A short man who McNear hadn't seen, dashed forward frantically waving his arms and screaming with a heavy French accent.

"Get down 'fore you scare 'em off," McNear responded in a stern whisper.

"I think your head, she's cracked," replied the Frenchman.

"My head? Why don't you keep yours quiet so I can plug the rest of 'em?"

"Why you shoot my camels?"

"Camels? I thought they were moose."

Tom McNear's error cost him several hundred dollars, that and a red face every time he entered a saloon and someone felt compelled to relate how the hunter had obtained his unusual nickname: Camel McNear.

In the 1860s the Frenchman's camels carried mining supplies across Idaho's panhandle to western Montana, where the hapless McNear mistook them for moose. The idea to use camels as pack animals had come from Jefferson Davis when he was Secretary of War.

In the late 1850s Davis imported 74 North African and Arabian dromedaries to supply the Army's western garrisons. In theory it seemed a good idea since camels could haul stores over grades that would break wagon teams of horses or mules. But like other bureaucratic theories that look good on paper, this one had its problems.

When confronting a camel on the trail, horses and mules recoiled as if they'd come face-to-face with a grizzly. Should a packer prod a camel too forcefully, he would likely end up combing a handful of pungent, green cud out of his beard. When they spit, camels have uncanny aim.

Eventually, the Army tired of Jefferson Davis's experiment and sold the camels to independent packers, who planned using them to supply the west's remote mines. A few animals eventually found their way to Idaho. Although the new owners did learn to tolerate the camels' touchy temperaments and their capacity to strike terror in more traditional pack stock, they never devised a means to protect the dromedaries' tender feet. Bred for desert sand, the camels quickly went lame when walking over rocky trails. Every trip required they be allowed to rest and mend, which is what the Frenchman's herd was doing when Tom McNear mistook them for moose.

By 1870 Idaho's camels had all but disappeared—for a second time. Beginning with the Miocene, nearly 24 million years ago, prehistoric camels thrived in an Idaho that was far more humid and lush than it is today. The animals lasted through the Pliocene Epoch as the state slowly became more arid. However, the ice ages of the Pleistocene led to their demise. They disappeared along with the woodland musk-ox and mastodon.

In 1959-60 Ruth Gruhn, a graduate student from Radcliffe College, unearthed evidence of Idaho's prehistoric camels. During her dig at Wilson Butte Cave, northwest of Eden, the young archaeologist determined that camels were hunted by man as recently as 10,500 years ago.

Wilson Butte Cave

Leave I-84 at Twin Falls Exit 173 and head north on US 93. In 5.6 miles turn east on Idaho State Road 25; in 9.2 miles at the state historical sign about the Minidoka Japanese Relocation Center turn left (north) on Hunt Road. In 4.3 miles turn left on Eden Road, which eventually changes from asphalt to dirt. **(Do not drive this road when it's wet!)** In 5.4 miles cross the North Side Canal; the piles of lava are from its excavation. Bear right at the cattle guard and continue another 2.6 miles. Swing left for 200 yards toward the prominent rocky mound, which is Wilson Butte Cave.

IDAHO'S
Camas War

The Treaty of 1868 assigned Idaho's Bannocks to the Fort Hall Indian Reservation, a swath of land along the Portneuf River. At that time, the reservation was about the size of Delaware and Rhode Island combined. The treaty also granted the Bannocks unrestricted access to the Camas Prairie near present-day Fairfield, Idaho.

Every spring, blue camas lilies carpeted this lush plain with flowers. For countless generations the Bannocks had harvested the onion-shaped camas bulbs when they matured in late summer. However, during the bureaucratic meandering that led to the treaty's ratification, Camas Prairie somehow became Kansas Prairie, which was a place that didn't exist. Still, the tribal elders were unconcerned. Their grandmothers' grandmothers had dug the nutritious bulbs, and the U.S. Government had given its word. The Camas Prairie belonged to the Bannocks, and they thought it always would.

In the 1870s the Army resettled Shoshones from Wyoming on the Fort Hall Reservation, compelling them to compete with the Bannocks for government rations. Federal bungling and indifference, compounded by graft, ensured the allotments were always less than what was promised. As Indian fathers watched their families go hungry, their resentment grew. Each year their unrest was fueled by the white farmers and miners who crowded into southeastern Idaho, overrunning the hunting grounds, wasting the deer and elk, killing the Indians' ponies for "sport," and tearing apart the earth with steel plows.

In 1877 Chief Buffalo Horn offered his Bannock scouts to General Howard in order to chase down the fleeing Nez Perce.

Blooming camas lily (Camassia Quamash). It's difficult to imagine that such a delicate flower could have ignited a bloody war.

When 40 Army horses were stolen, Howard blamed the Bannocks, jailing several. Although Buffalo Horn proclaimed his scouts' innocence, Howard refused to free the prisoners until the animals were returned.

Buffalo Horn quit the Army in disgust, retiring to the Fort Hall Reservation. Throughout that autumn and winter, the chief railed against the white man's injustice. He was especially contemptuous of the Army, citing Custer's defeat by the Sioux in 1876 and General Howard's humiliating campaign against the Nez Perce as examples of how inept the troopers were in battle. To the angry warriors who listened, Buffalo Horn's call for revenge struck a chord.

In May 1878 settlers taking advantage of the "Kansas Prairie" clerical error herded hogs onto the Bannocks' Camas Prairie. The hogs quickly uprooted and ate the succulent bulbs. A week or so later when Buffalo Horn and some of the tribe visited the prairie, they were appalled at the destruction. After Bill Silvey, Lew Kensler, and George Nesbit drove a large herd of cattle and horses onto the plain, Indian tempers reached a boil.

On May 28 two Bannocks rode into Silvey's camp as the stockmen were finishing breakfast. Whether or not the warriors planned to fight or were provoked is lost to history, but one of the Indians drew his revolver and shot Nesbit in the mouth, severing his tongue. As Kensler lunged for his rifle, a bullet grazed his scalp. At a spring a few yards away, Silvey dove for cover as more shots dusted the dirt near his feet. Ignoring his bleeding head, Kensler fired his Winchester as the Bannocks sprinted for their horses. He thought he wounded one, but he wasn't certain.

Needing a doctor for Nesbit, the stockmen rode to another cow camp about 16 miles away. From there other gallopers raced to inform the Army at Fort Boise.

Meanwhile, a dozen or more Bannocks plundered the Silvey camp, driving off 15 horses. Around a council fire that night, Buffalo Horn persuaded 200 of his tribesmen to follow him on the warpath. Southern Idaho ignited like dry tinder.

At Glenns Ferry the Indians crossed the Snake River and then cut the ferrymen's boat lines. A few miles away the warriors came on some freight wagons that were returning from Nevada. The Bannocks killed the three teamsters and looted the wagons, which contained several jugs of whiskey. As the war party celebrated its victory, a Bannock named Bruneau John decided he'd had enough fighting. Leaving his companions to consume the liquor, he rode to Bruneau Valley and warned the settlers to flee. When Buffalo Horn's warriors finally reached the area, they found nothing but empty homesteads.

On May 31 telegrams alerted General Howard's headquarters in Portland, Oregon. By early June Army posts throughout the territory were dispatching soldiers to quell what everyone feared would be a general uprising. From Fort Boise Captain Reuben Bernard led a cavalry troop after Buffalo Horn, while Idaho's most famous lawman, Orlando "Rube" Robbins, brought along 35 volunteer scouts.

After learning the Bannocks were raiding the nearby countryside, 26 miners from Silver City in Owyhee County confronted Buffalo Horn and 60 warriors near South Mountain. The miners attacked on horseback, but the well-hidden Indians held their ground. Outgunned, the white militia attempted to withdraw, prompting the chief to counterattack. Just when it appeared Buffalo Horn would win a great victory, an "unlucky" shot took his life. Distracted by their leader's death, the Bannocks allowed the miners to escape. The chastened militia scurried home to Silver City in time to see Captain Bernard arrive with his soldiers.

On June 12 General Howard reached Fort Boise, determined to prevent another humiliation similar to the one he'd suffered at the hands of the Nez Perce. Soon telegraph wires across the entire region hummed with urgent messages summoning troops.

After the battle with the miners near South Mountain, the Bannocks headed to eastern Oregon, where other tribes joined the campaign to recapture their lost homeland. A Paiute war chief named Egan now became the nominal leader. Meanwhile, Captain Bernard's command left Silver City and trailed after the hostiles. Some days the troopers covered 50 miles. As June was ending the Captain located the Indians' camp, (according to Army estimates) bustling with 2,000 men, women, and children. That night a handful of scouts under Rube Robbins launched a furious sneak attack against the sleeping tribes. Panicked, the Indians fled directly into Bernard's blocking force of 250 cavalrymen.

During the melee, which continued until after dawn, Chief Egan spotted Robbins. In a confrontation reminiscent of the days of chivalry, the two raging warriors charged each other with their guns blazing. The Paiute hung off the side of his horse, firing from under its neck, while Robbins sat upright in his saddle. Their duel ended when Robbins shattered Egan's wrist with a bullet.

After both sides withdrew to lick their wounds, the Army counted five dead, the Indians nearly 100. For the next couple of days, Captain Bernard rested his exhausted troopers and awaited the arrival of General Howard. The pause allowed the Indians to slip away.

In July the soldiers fought the Indians to a standoff in Oregon's Blue Mountains. Again the hostiles escaped. Then a few days later other troops caught them near Pendleton, Oregon, handing the warriors a crushing defeat.

Each surviving band now raced for the security of its own reservation. With four companies of cavalry in pursuit, the Bannocks returned to Idaho, pillaging homesteads along the way. After reaching Fort Hall, the warriors melded with those who hadn't left. Although the Army sought no additional reprisals, it never again allowed the Bannocks to dig roots on the Camas Prairie.

Camas *(Camassia quamash)* belongs to the lily family. Ranging from southern British Columbia to northern California and eastward into northern Utah, Wyoming, Montana, and Idaho, it prefers moist meadows. During the spring, its star-shaped flowers paint entire fields in blue and violet.

When harvested in August, camas bulbs are odorless and resemble tiny white onions. Indians baked the bulbs in holes, layering them from bottom to top with hot stones, grass and alder leaves, camas bulbs, more grass and alder leaves, soil, and fire. After three days, the bulbs were removed and dried. Prepared this way, they could be stored for three years.

Cooked camas roots are brown and smell like dried fruit. They taste slightly sweet. For a special treat, Indians enjoyed eating roasted bulbs dipped in beef or buffalo marrow. The bulbs were used in soups and baked into camas bread. Lewis and Clark reported eating a few loaves during their journeys across northern Idaho. Indians also made a soothing cough syrup by boiling cooked camas in water and mixing the resulting juice with honey.

Idaho's Camas Prairie at the foot of the Soldier Mountains.

SIGHTS TO SEE

Camas Prairie Centennial Marsh (near where the attack on Silvey's camp occurred)

If you approach from the east, drive nine miles west from Fairfield on US 20. At the sign for the Centennial Marsh turn left on Wolf Lane. The one-lane road out to the observation point lies eight miles beyond. This narrow track to the center of the marsh is occasionally flooded during the spring runoff. Good gravel roads lead around the marsh, returning to US 20 at Hill City.

If you're coming from the west, take I-84 Exit 95 near Mountain Home and follow US 20 east. At Hill City ignore the sign for the marsh and continue on US 20 for another five miles, turning right on Wolf Lane and then follow the directions given above.

Depending on the year's snowfall, mid-May through mid-June is usually the best time to see the camas in full bloom. During the nesting season, the marsh is alive with waterfowl and shorebirds, including mallards, pintails, cinnamon teals, shovelers, sandhill cranes, curlews, and avocets, to name but a few.

ORLANDO "RUBE" ROBBINS

An Idaho Paladin

Deadwood, Tombstone, Dodge City—each of these towns evokes the image of America's frontier, where men such as Wild Bill Hickok, Bat Masterson, and the Earp brothers held sway with their six-guns and tin stars. First the dime novels and then Hollywood westerns immortalized these pistoleers, gilding their reputations until fact melded with fantasy.

Idaho, too, had its "Wyatt Earp." Though forgotten by a world that learns its history from the movies, Orlando "Rube" Robbins was every bit as much the bold lawman as were his more famous contemporaries.

Rube Robbins was born in Maine on August 30, 1836. As a teenager he owned a yoke of oxen, which his father sold without his son's permission. Infuriated, the 17-year-old Robbins walked away from his family's farm and headed for the mining camps of California.

At the age of 25 he left California and drifted to the gold strikes in northern Idaho. Then two years later in August 1863, he moved to the diggings at Idaho City. The following year he became a deputy sheriff.

The Civil War polarized the hardened miners of Idaho City. Yankee and Rebel sympathizers often settled their political differences with their fists or knives. Many a night Robbins had to wade into a drunken melee in order to compel the peace.

Early one summer a number of southerners boasted they wouldn't permit any Yankees to sing the *Star Spangled Banner* on Independence Day. When Robbins heard the bluster, he became incensed. He was a Union man to the core. On July 4 he walked into a saloon filled with southerners. Without saying a word, he hopped atop a billiard table and drew his two revolvers. The raucous crowd immediately fell silent as every eye fixed on his Colts.

"Oh, say can you see by the dawn's early light. . . ?"

Not a person moved as Robbins's voice filled the barroom with the song's three-quarter time.

". . . O'er the land of the free and the home of the brave?"

After finishing the final note, the young deputy holstered his pistols, climbed down from the table, and stepped into the street. No one tried to stop him.

Robbins's repute as a lawman soon carried him to Boise City, where he worked as a deputy sheriff and later as a U.S. marshal. In March 1868 an underground gunfight erupted in Silver City between miners employed by the Golden Chariot and Elmore Mines. Known as the Owyhee War, this 100-man battle started when the Golden Chariot's miners tunneled into a shaft belonging to the Elmore.

The subterranean shootout lasted three days before Idaho's territorial governor sent Robbins to force a truce. The deputy rode from Boise to Silver City in six hours, amazingly fast, considering that the 60 or so miles of roads he covered were no doubt mud-cloaked from the spring rains and snowmelt. Robbins wasted no time bringing the warring factions together. By sundown the day he arrived he had negotiated an end to the fray.

During Idaho's Indian Wars Robbins served as head of scouts and a colonel in the territorial militia. The Camas War of the late 1870s found Robbins pursuing Chief Egan and his Paiute and Bannock warriors through the Owyhee badlands near South Mountain. At Silver Creek Robbins and Egan fought perhaps the most bizarre "duel" since the days of Arthurian chivalry.

According to a militia eyewitness, Robbins and four of his command were riding over a ridge when they were surprised by a band of Indians. The scouts spurred their horses, trying to get away as the warriors took up the chase. When a scout name Bill Myers was wounded and his horse killed, Robbins turned back to rescue him.

As Robbins galloped toward Myers, he spotted Chief Egan, who also recognized the famed lawman. Like two knights errant having been whisked from a medieval time, the colonel and chief began jousting with their Winchesters. As their horses circled each other, these fearless paladins blasted away, oblivious to every other

Orlando "Rube" Robbins. Courtesy of Idaho Historical Society.

fight except their own.

When their rifles were empty, they drew their pistols. Chief Egan's lead tore through Robbins's clothes and nicked his finger. Robbins's bullets also missed their mark as the chief deftly used his horse's neck for cover. And then a lucky shot hit Egan in the wrist, spilling him off his horse. Stunned, the chief had just crawled to his feet when trooper Myers wounded him in the chest.

While Egan's band carried off their fallen leader, Robbins pulled the injured scout up behind his saddle, and they raced toward the Army's lines.

Seven weeks later Robbins again proved his mettle. He was rowing Lieutenant W.R. Parnell, a bugler, and two cavalrymen across the Snake River when a horse they had tied behind their skiff panicked. Just as the men cut the animal loose, its thrashing capsized the boat. Parnell and the bugler began swimming while Robbins boosted one of the cavalrymen atop the overturned hull. The other cavalryman grabbed the horse's tail and was towed to shore.

Seeing the bugler begin to tire, Robbins left the safety of the rowboat and helped him to the shallows. Meanwhile, Lieutenant Parnell started to founder, weighted down by his boots, pistol, and cartridge belt. Robbins again plunged into the current, reaching Parnell as he was about to drown. Struggling against the current, Robbins kept the officer afloat until another boat came to their aid.

Throughout the 1870s, '80s, and '90s, Robbins tracked badmen across southern Idaho. In February 1876 after six bandits robbed the Silver City stagecoach on the outskirts of Boise, the deputy had them behind bars within two days of their crime. In August 1882 he covered 1,280 miles in 13 days before catching the outlaw Charlie Chambers. The few desperadoes who evaded Robbins's grasp counted themselves fortunate.

Yet there existed a side to Rube Robbins apart from gunplay and daring. In his 30s he joined the temperance movement and found religion. After his public baptism in the Boise River, he became president of the Methodist Church Sunday School. He won a term in the Idaho Territorial Legislature, and a few years afterwards, he served as its Sergeant at Arms.

In his late 60s Robbins escorted prisoners to the state penitentiary. Although many of them were one-third his age, none ever escaped.

On May 1, 1908, Idaho's greatest lawman died of a heart attack. After his death, tributes poured forth, each trying to take his measure. Few came close to the praise uttered years earlier by Cherokee Bob.

As the outlaw lay dying from Robbins's gunshot, he said the marshal never jumped to the side after squeezing the trigger but "always sprang through the smoke [of his revolver] and advanced upon his opponent, firing as he came."

Catholic Church in Silver City, Idaho's most famous ghost town.

Silver City (the "Queen" of Idaho's ghost towns)

Take the I-84 business route into Mountain Home, turning west on Idaho State Road 67. Near the entrance to the U.S. Air Force base, go right at the sign for Grand View. At the intersection with Idaho State Road 78 turn right (northwest) and drive 25 miles. Go left onto Silver City Road at the state historical markers. Silver City lies 20 miles away.

Silver City Road is suitable for cars, but vehicles towing trailers are not advised. The road is normally open from June through October. Start with a full gas tank as no fuel is available in town.

In its prime, Silver City boasted a population of 2,500. Now summer residents swell the town to 300. Only a handful of people, however, live here year-round.

During the second weekend in September, Silver City hosts an open house, offering tours through its historic buildings.

PEG LEG ANNIE
of Rocky Bar

During the early 1860s prospectors began scouring Idaho's Boise Mountains for gold. As they combed the creeks feeding the Feather River, a few of them discovered the mother lode. Within months the strike brought miners streaming into the rugged terrain. In their wake flocked gamblers, laundresses, saloonkeepers, and merchants. Almost overnight, clapboard cabins sprang up on a gravel bench dubbed Rocky Bar.

On Independence Day 1864 Stephen McIntyre came to the fledgling town in search of his fortune. Beside him walked his wife and son, while perched atop his shoulders rode his four-year-old daughter, Felicia Ann—or Annie, as her family called her.

The ore was rich, and Annie's father prospered, eventually becoming part-owner of the Golden Star Mine.

Rocky Bar also flourished, though its muddy streets seemed as rough as the outlying country. Drunken brawls were commonplace. Arguments over card games, rebel sympathizers wanting to refight the Civil War, often just plain orneriness led men to settle their differences with knuckles and guns. The cause is lost to history, but in one of these mindless melees, Stephen McIntyre was shot dead.

During the 1870s the surface mines played out, and the fast-money operators left for fresher diggings. All those who didn't move on wondered if Rocky Bar would wither away like Idaho's other boom-to-bust mining towns.

Annie stayed at the Bar and grew into an attractive young woman, pretty enough to interest Tom Morrow, who married her when she was 14. He died several years later, leaving her with a son. (Some reports say she had five children.)

During the 1880s Annie supported herself with a boarding house and restaurant. Then in mid-decade, English investors revived Rocky Bar, infusing capital to expand mines such as the

Elmore. The miners returned, too, many sleeping under Annie's roof and eating the meals she set on her dining table. Those down on their luck knew they'd never go hungry so long as Annie had the strength to fire up her stove.

Throughout the 1880s and into the '90s Annie was a fixture of the town. When her coarse language couldn't quell a ruckus, her revolver did. She shot holes in her eatery's ceiling more than once in an effort to quiet some drunken loudmouth. Yet despite Annie's lack of gentility, everyone knew her heart held more gold than had ever been panned from Rocky Bar's many streams.

In the spring of 1896 Annie and Emma Soaper (some reports call her Dutch Em Von Losch) hiked 14 miles to the sister town of Atlanta. On May 15 they began their journey home in a snowstorm.

Later that day the mail packer, Will Tate, left Atlanta for Bald Mountain, where he intended exchanging pouches with the mail carrier coming from Rocky Bar. Five miles south of town Tate caught up with the two women.

Despite the storm Annie and Emma assured him they would be fine. Giggling, they told him they had fortified themselves with whiskey and felt quite warm.

After advising them to follow the prints left by his snowshoes, Tate bid them good-bye. By the time he reached the mail packers' cabin near the summit of Bald Mountain, the storm had become a blizzard.

Tate swapped pouches with the Rocky Bar carrier and started his return-trek to Atlanta. His tracks from a few hours before were buried under several inches of snow. Although he didn't see Annie and Emma along the road, he wasn't particularly worried, figuring they must have turned back to wait for fair weather.

After reaching town, Tate inquired about the women, but no one had seen them. He now realized they must be lost.

The blizzard continued for two more days, forestalling any rescue attempt. The moment the sky cleared, a relief party set out on snowshoes.

When the rescuers found the women, Emma was dead. For some reason her frozen body was wrapped in Annie's undergarments. Snow-blind and out of her head, Annie was crawling about on her hands and knees. Ominously, her feet were severely frostbitten.

The searchers carried Annie to Atlanta and then sent word to Mountain Home for a doctor. Meanwhile Annie's ankles and feet swelled, turning black and gangrenous. The miners knew she couldn't hold out until the doctor arrived. Unless her legs were amputated, she would die.

The miners gave their feeble friend as much whiskey as she could drink, and then tied her down atop a table. Someone suggested they draw straws to see who would perform the operation, but Tug Wilson volunteered. Using a knife and a meat saw, he severed Annie's legs a few inches above her ankles.

In time Annie returned to Rocky Bar. After her stumps healed, artificial legs enabled her again to serve meals to her boarders.

Shortly after the turn of the century, she began living with Henry Longheme, who owned a saloon adjacent to her rooming house. In 1924 he took her life savings—$12,000— to deposit in a San Francisco bank. Annie never again saw Longheme or her money.

Soon thereafter the gold petered out and Rocky Bar's miners drifted away. Peg Leg Annie also moved on and ultimately outlasted the town. When she died in Mountain Home at the age of 75, Rocky Bar was nothing but a fading memory.

The history of Peg Leg Annie has grown into legend. Although there are as many versions of her life as there are story tellers, all speak of her warm heart.

In May 1996 on the 100th anniversary of Annie's amputation, the residents of Atlanta, Idaho, commemorated her ordeal with a "leg roast." According to a long-time local named Dennis, Annie was toasted during a delicious dinner that featured leg of lamb.

Rocky Bar, where Peg Leg Annie once gave free meals to miners down on their luck.

"Peg Leg" Annie Morrow.
Courtesy of Idaho Historical Society.

SIGHTS TO SEE

Rocky Bar

From Fairfield drive 25 miles west on US 20 and turn north on the Pine-Featherville Road. This paved highway leads 28 miles to Featherville and passes the picturesque Anderson Ranch Reservoir. North of the reservoir, the road winds alongside the South Fork of the Boise River, a fly fisherman's dream. Between the reservoir and Featherville are numerous campgrounds and several motel-resorts, which have gas and food. Fifty yards beyond the Featherville Motel veer left on the unnamed gravel road (FR 156). Rocky Bar is 7½ miles away.

As you look at the few remaining buildings, their sideboards weathered by the sun and rain, imagine the town as it was in the late 1860s when it bustled with 2,500 people.

Atlanta

In Rocky Bar turn right on James Creek Road, which climbs over Bald Mountain. Although steep and ***not* advised for trailers**, the grade is passable for cars. In 13½ miles turn right on Middle Fork Road for another 1½ miles.

Atlanta supports about 40 full-time residents and during the author's last visit it had a store and restaurant/bar.

Carlin party. Courtesy of Idaho Historical Society.

THE CARLIN DISASTER

"The Clearwater Mountains are an elk hunter's dream," William Carlin told his two friends as they departed Weippe, Idaho, on September 20, 1893. Martin Spencer, their guide, as much as guaranteed they would find trophy-sized bulls. Whether or not they could kill something suitable for mounting depended upon their skill with their rifles. With George Colgate, their 52-year-old cook, bringing up the rear, the small hunting party was in high spirits as it rode east into the foothills and picked up the Lolo Trail.

Native Americans had traveled this trace for generations before Lewis and Clark made it famous. In 1866 the Department of the Interior sought to turn it into a road, but surveyors deemed the country too rough. Eleven years later, General Howard chased Chief Joseph and 700 Nez Perce over its precipitous contours. The Indians escaped, but the dead horses sacrificed by them and the pursuing troopers testified to the route's difficulty.

For the Carlin party, the trail's reputation merely heightened the adventure. When it snowed early in the trip, what should have been a warning was ignored in the excitement of shooting grouse and hooking trout. The men pushed on, forcing their stock over a frozen path increasingly choked with deadfall. Each mile involved a tiring climb and steep descent.

On September 26 they quit the Lolo Trail and dropped down to the Lochsa River. That afternoon they stumbled upon the half-finished cabin of Jerry Johnson and Ben Keeley, two prospectors who intended spending the winter in the Clearwater wilderness. Johnson warned Carlin that he and his friends ought to get out of the mountains before the passes filled with snow, but the advice went unheeded.

The following morning Colgate begged off his chores, complaining that it hurt him to walk. For years an enlarged prostate had required him to drain his bladder artificially. Embarrassed to perform the procedure before strangers, he had purposely left his catheter at home. Still, he assured everyone that he'd be fine if he was allowed to rest.

Annoyed but not overly concerned with their cook's deteriorating health, the hunters spent the next two weeks missing or wounding more elk than they killed. Most every day it snowed. Meanwhile, uremic poison ballooned Colgate's legs to double their normal size.

At their guide's insistence, the hunters grudgingly agreed to leave their camp on October 10. They headed for the Lolo Trail, but their horses soon floundered in the deep snow. After returning to the Johnson-Keeley cabin, the party faced its plight. Colgate's condition was worsening by the hour. If the cook didn't get to a doctor, he would soon die. He was too weak to snowshoe, and the others hadn't the strength to drag him in a sled, especially over such an uncompromising route. Their only hope lay with the Lochsa River.

Carlin hired Keeley to build two 26-foot rafts and pilot them downstream. The journey began on November 3. In the first hour the raft carrying Colgate broke apart in the rapids. The men fished the cook and their supplies out of the freezing torrent and loaded them on the second boat.

For nine days the party battled channel-clogging boulders and white water, while Colgate continued to deteriorate. Each new mile seemed to bring rapids worse than in the one before. Then at Holly Creek the river won. The men discarded their raft. To attempt floating farther meant suicide.

The cook was now so ill he didn't know his own name. Unable to carry him and deeming his condition terminal, the party parceled out its remaining food and continued on foot, leaving Colgate to die.

The steep canyon reduced the pace to a crawl. Some days the men covered only a mile; five they considered cause for celebration. With their rations nearly gone, they searched for game but saw little and shot less. The few trout they caught barely kept them from starving.

Finally on November 22, near the Hellgate Rapids, the

exhausted survivors met a rescue party that had been dispatched by Carlin's worried father. Thanksgiving Day found Carlin and his friends enjoying a sumptuous dinner in Kendrick.

No sooner did the newspapers announce the men were safe than a public outcry attacked them for deserting George Colgate. The paltry $25 William Carlin gave Colgate's widow merely fueled the criticism.

The following summer Colgate's bones were located eight miles downstream from where he'd been abandoned, seemingly washed there by the spring floods. They were buried near Johnson's cabin at a game lick now dubbed Colgate Warm Springs.

Lochsa River

This "wild and scenic" river can be approached from Lewiston via US 12 or on Idaho State Road 13 from Grangeville to Kooskia, where the state road intersects US 12. From Kooskia follow US 12 east along the Middle Fork of the Clearwater River for 23 miles to Lowell where you'll come to the mouth of the Lochsa. From here US 12 parallels the Lochsa for about 70 miles until the river bends south near the Powell Ranger Station.

The Lochsa River is a playground for trout fisherman and white water rafters, alike. As you drive past the roaring rapids, imagine trying to run them in winter conditions aboard a crude log raft as did the Carlin Party.

Colgate Warm Springs and George Colgate's Grave

The Colgate Licks National Recreation Trail is located 61 miles east of Lowell and may be accessed from US 12. The trail leads north from the parking area to the springs. With luck you may see elk or deer licking the mineral-laden water. George Colgate's grave is on the east side of the parking area, a bit below the highway.

THE LEGAL SAGA
of Diamondfield Jack

In the mid-1890s Idaho's Cassia County stretched west past Salmon Falls Creek to the Owyhee County line. This grassy expanse of south-central Idaho belonged to the cattle ranchers and sheepherders.

A shaky peace existed between the beef and wool barons, its enforcement bolstered by a "deadline" that split Cassia County along the high ground forming its center. The cattle grazed west of this boundary; the sheep ranged east.

When the sheepherders began encroaching in the summer of 1895, the Sparks-Harrell Company, which owned cattle ranches in Idaho and Nevada, hired Jackson Lee Davis as a night rider. His duties were explicit: drive the sheep beyond the deadline.

A miner turned gunman, Davis acquired his "Diamondfield" nickname because he had once prospected for diamonds.

Diamondfield Jack began confronting the sheep ranchers with his Winchester. Before long, most considered it healthier keeping to their own range. However, in November he wounded a sheepherder who had strayed onto Sparks-Harrell land. With the county sheriff in the wool growers' pocket, Davis deemed it safer retreating to Wells, Nevada, until things quieted. His absence soon emboldened the sheep ranchers to intrude past the deadline.

In late January 1896 Davis again visited a Sparks-Harrell ranch in southern Idaho. On February 1 he and another night rider, Fred Gleason, shot it out with herders a few miles from the property. Although no one was hit, the incident prompted the gunfighters to hightail it south. They left the ranch at dawn February 4, pausing for noon dinner at another of the company's ranch outposts just below the state line.

On February 16 two sheepherders were found shot to death on Deep Creek. They'd been murdered the same day Diamondfield Jack and Fred Gleason departed for Nevada. Having few clues other than a corncob pipe and the night riders' reputations, the Albion sheriff issued warrants for the two Sparks-Harrell gunmen.

A year passed before Diamondfield Jack came to trial in Albion, which was located in the heart of sheep country. The Idaho Wool Growers Association hired William Borah to assist the prosecutor, and the Sparks-Harrell Company retained James Hawley for the defense.

The prosecution's witnesses said Diamondfield Jack had bragged about shooting sheepherders in Idaho. Whether his drunken boasts pertained to earlier skirmishes or the murders on Deep Creek, a jury of sheep sympathizers was to decide. The defense argued the accused couldn't possibly have ridden from the Sparks-Harrell ranch to the murder site with enough time to eat noon dinner in Nevada, a distance of 55 miles. On April 15, 1897, the jury rendered its verdict: first-degree murder. The judge sentenced Diamondfield Jack to hang.

While Davis awaited execution, the state tried Fred Gleason. After hearing the same evidence that had convicted Diamondfield Jack the jury incredibly found Gleason not guilty.

Defense attorney Hawley then enlisted two cowboys to make the alleged murder-ride. Although they did it in 5½ hours, both attested it would take longer in winter. On this basis Hawley obtained a stay of execution while he appealed. In June 1898 the Idaho Supreme Court sustained the original verdict. Diamondfield Jack's appointment with the hangman was set for October 21.

Eight days before the execution, Jim Bower, a Sparks-Harrell ranch superintendent, and his friend, Jeff Gray, signed affidavits, admitting to the killings. Bower said the corncob pipe found at the murder scene was his. Despite these confessions, the Idaho Board of Pardons refused to release Diamondfield Jack. Instead, it merely postponed his date with the gallows until December 16, and at the last minute delayed it again until February 1, 1899.

Hawley now appealed in federal court, which issued another stay. Riders brought the injunction to the Albion jail only hours before Davis was set to swing.

A few days later a new law requiring that all executions take place in the Idaho State Penitentiary sent Diamondfield Jack to

Jack Davis a.k.a. "Diamondfield Jack." Courtesy of Idaho Historical Society.

death row in Boise. Then in December the Idaho Supreme Court reversed the law, remanding him to Albion.

Meanwhile, the Cassia County District Court ruled that Bower and Gray had acted in self-defense, acquitting them of murdering the same sheepherders Davis had been convicted of killing.

In late 1900 Diamondfield Jack's case reached the U.S. Supreme Court, which because of procedural technicalities refused to intervene. Hawley then petitioned Cassia County for a new trial, but the district judge denied the request. The trip to the hangman was rescheduled for June 21, 1901.

During this time many letters begging clemency arrived at the Idaho Board of Pardons, whose members had recently changed. The Board put off the execution twice more as it granted a review, the latter reprieve coming as the Albion townsfolk gathered around the gallows.

On July 16, 1901, the Board added a final irony to this legal farce, commuting Diamondfield Jack's death sentence to life imprisonment. Davis moved back to the state prison in Boise.

Again Hawley appealed to the Idaho Supreme Court, and once more it refused to release his client. Next the attorney re-solicited the Board of Pardons. The arguments and depositions continued until December 18, 1902, when at long last Diamondfield Jack walked free.

Jack Davis relocated to Tonopah, Nevada, and struck it rich prospecting for gold; however, his newfound wealth soon slipped through his fingers. From 1908 until 1948 little is known of his whereabouts, although he was reportedly seen in Mexico, Montana, New York City, and California.

December 1948 found Diamondfield Jack in Las Vegas. Drunk or sober, no one knows for sure, he stepped off a sidewalk into the path of an oncoming taxicab. Five days later on January 2, 1949, the former night rider finally met his maker when he died from his injuries in a Nevada hospital.

Old Idaho State Penitentiary, where Diamondfield Jack awaited the hangman's noose.

SIGHTS TO SEE

Old Idaho Penitentiary

From Boise I-84 Exit 54 take Broadway Ave. north three miles. Turn right on Warm Springs Ave. for 1½ miles, and then go left on Old Penitentiary Road. The prison offers daily tours except on state holidays.

Old Cassia County Courthouse

From I-84 Exit 216, which is nine miles east of Burley, drive 12 miles south on Idaho State Road 77 to Albion. The old courthouse sits at the corner of Main and Market Streets. The trial was held on the second floor. A Diamondfield Jack historical sign is in the village park alongside State Road 77.

The ranch from which Diamondfield Jack rode that fateful February morning now lies beneath the Salmon Falls Creek Reservoir, just north of Jackpot, Nevada.

Blue Lakes, site of Ira Perrine's farm.

THE CAREY ACT

A "Magic" Law

The Homestead Act of 1862 offered land to any man or woman willing to scratch a living from 160 acres of western dirt. The Desert Land Act of 1877 allowed a homesteader in arid regions to settle a complete section—640 acres—provided the intrepid pioneer irrigated the holding within three years.

On the parched Idaho plain high above the Snake River, such a task would have taken a millionaire's purse and millionaires didn't homestead. During the 19th century south-central Idaho belonged only to the sagebrush and rattlesnakes.

In 1883 Ira "I. B." Perrine left Indiana, hoping to make his fortune in the silver mines of Idaho's Wood River Valley. After realizing he could earn more money feeding the miners than in working beside them digging ore, the lanky young Hoosier acquired a small herd of dairy cattle and began selling milk and butter.

During the autumn of 1884 Perrine drove his herd south for the winter, pasturing it in a grassy nook alongside the Snake River. Over the next decade and a half, this energetic entrepreneur built a thriving farm where today sits the Blue Lakes Country Club of Twin Falls. Watered by spring-fed pools, the fertile volcanic soil grew fruits and vegetables for the mining camps of Hailey and Ketchum.

In 1894 Wyoming's Senator Joseph Carey spearheaded a bill through Congress that allotted any western state one million acres to be sold in 40- to 160-acre plots. Priced at 50¢ per acre, the parcels had to be irrigated within 10 years. Yielding to the fact that few millionaires were likely to line up in order to provide the necessary financing for large irrigation projects, the Carey Act allowed states to license private companies to build and manage them.

Ira Perrine reasoned if water could make his Blue Lakes property thrive it could also do so for the sagebrush-dotted plain. Accordingly, he envisioned a land teeming with lush farms. In 1900 he persuaded Stanley Milner, a Utah banker, to fund an irrigation survey. The study proved Perrine's dream feasible.

Perrine next enlisted a mining broker who had ties to eastern money. Using the financier as his go-between, the plucky Hoosier sold his scheme to Frank Buhl and Peter Kimberly, Pennsylvania steel barons.

Backed by these wealthy investors, Perrine and Milner formed the Twin Falls Land and Water Company. A Chicago investment bank then raised the additional funds needed to dig irrigation canals and build a dam across the Snake River.

The State of Idaho granted the Twin Falls Land and Water Company the right to develop 244,000 acres. In 1903 workers broke ground for Milner Dam, launching the South Side Project. Meanwhile other crews began excavating the Low Line Canal south of the Snake River.

The following year the company platted the town of Twin Falls. When the land office started selling parcels, however, only a handful of people stepped forward to buy.

The lack of enthusiasm changed with the completion of Milner Dam. When Frank Buhl shut the floodgates on March 1, 1905, diverting water into the Low Line Canal, would-be farmers flocked to the land office. City dwellers came too, swelling Twin Falls into a boomtown. Soon other communities sprang up along the man-made waterway, including two named for the original investors: Buhl and Kimberly.

It seemed as if overnight the countryside south of the Snake River blossomed as though it had been struck by a wizard's wand. It became known as Magic Valley.

After Frank Buhl and Peter Kimberly declined to back a similar undertaking north of the Snake River, the Kuhn family of Pittsburgh took their place. But from the start the North Side Project was beset by problems.

In 1913 a nationwide financial panic threatened to dry up capital. As the Kuhns' fortune dwindled in the plummeting stock market, Perrine scrambled to keep his work crews paid.

When a planned reservoir north of the Snake River succumbed to the porous volcanic soil, Milner Dam proved unable

to make up the shortfall in water. Perrine again saved the day by persuading the U.S. Reclamation Service to dam Jackson Lake in Wyoming (now part of Grand Teton National Park). The additional water was a godsend during southern Idaho's torrid summers.

The North Side Project eventually brought irrigation to 185,000 acres. By the 1920s one man's vision had become a showcase for the Carey Act. Through dogged determination, Ira Perrine had transformed the central Snake River Plain into an agricultural mecca that is truly magical.

Milner Dam

From I-84 Exit 194, about 20 miles east of Twin Falls and 30 miles west of the I-84/I-86 interchange, drive south three miles on Ridgeway Road and turn east on Power Line Road. After two miles when you merge with Milner Road, keep right. The dam is two miles farther.

Centennial Waterfront Park

In Twin Falls drive north on Blue Lakes Boulevard (US 93). After crossing Pole Line Road, continue 0.1 mile farther and turn west at the sign for Centennial Waterfront Park. If coming from the north, the turn is 0.4 mile south of the Perrine Bridge. Follow the road as it curves right toward the river; 100 yards later, a street sign will show you are on Canyon Springs Road. Continue for one mile as the road descends into the Snake River Canyon. Swing right at the small sign marking the park entrance.

Numerous trails lead along the Snake River, presenting stunning views of the Perrine Bridge and the basalt-layered canyon. Although Ira Perrine eventually farmed the bottomland on both sides of the river, he located his home near the aquifer-fed lakes on the north shore, which is the present site of the Blue Lakes Country Club.

Perrine Bridge

Located 0.5 mile north of Twin Falls on US 93. The visitor center parking lot on the south side provides access to the bridge walkways and the north and south rim overlooks.

Named for Ira Perrine, the Perrine Bridge was built in 1976, replacing an older span of the same name. It is over 0.25 mile long and arches 486 feet above the water, offering a panorama of the Snake River Gorge that is nothing short of spectacular.

IDAHO'S
Lineage of Fire

Saturday, August 20, 1910, dawned hot. In Wallace, Idaho, the sun came up orange, its rays diffused by a brownish-gray veil which overhung the sky like an opaque screen. Out-of-doors the faint, southwest wind smelled of smoke.

The dry, sweltering summer had witnessed numerous fires throughout Idaho's panhandle. That Saturday a fair-sized one scorched the woods a dozen miles south of town. In the rugged terrain northeast of Elsie Peak, Ed Pulaski, a ranger with the young U.S. Forest Service, supervised crews across several miles of the fire's front.

Near mid-morning the wind gained strength, sending charcoal-colored smoke and gray ash over the Northern Pacific Railroad Depot. Downtown Wallace darkened as if in an eclipse.

At noon the tinderbox forests to the south and west exploded in flame, kindled by the growing wind. The fire raced down hillsides, jumped creeks and gullies, and then shot up the opposing slopes. Preheated by the torrid air, acres of timber ignited as if doused with gasoline.

Cut off by the blaze, Ed Pulaski ushered his men into a mining tunnel. Then while flames lapped at the entrance, he draped the opening with water-soaked blankets.

Smoke filled the shaft, forcing all but Pulaski on their bellies, their noses and mouths masked with wet rags. Using his hat for a bucket, Pulaski repeatedly flung water at the blankets to keep them from burning. Hour after hour he toiled until exhaustion and smoke finally brought him to his knees, unconscious.

Near dawn a fresh breeze announced that the fire had passed. Awakening from their would-be tomb, Pulaski and his men stumbled toward Wallace, leaving five of their number dead from smoke inhalation. All about, the land smoldered, its lush green trees reduced to blackened snags.

At the town limit, Pulaski's crew saw that Wallace too had not escaped. One-third of its buildings—100 structures—lay in ruin.

The Great Fire of 1910 killed 85 people. For two days, August 20 and 21, it consumed the Idaho and Montana countryside as if hell had been set loose on earth. By early September, its drifting smoke darkened Denver, Chicago, and Boston. Although President Taft called out the Army to help the fledgling Forest Service, it was the end of the month before rain brought the flames to heel.

Idaho saw 1.7 million acres—an area 2½ times the size of Rhode Island—go up in smoke. The lumber losses reached billions of board feet.

Today the Woodlawn Cemetery in St. Maries bears testament to the Great Fire's human cost. At the back of the graveyard is a circle of stones, marking the graves of 57 firefighters who burned to death near the St. Joe River.

Old fire damage and new growth in Idaho's panhandle.

SIGHTS TO SEE

Wallace

Located 47 miles east of Coeur d'Alene; use I-90 Exits 61 or 62. A tourist favorite, the town's historical center celebrates its early 20th-century mining heritage. The old train depot is at Pine and 6th Streets.

Woodlawn Cemetery

St. Maries sits at the junction of Idaho State Roads 3 and 5, about 55 miles southeast of Coeur d'Alene. The Woodlawn Cemetery is on W. Main Ave. (which is State Road 5) at 23rd St. The firefighters' memorial occupies the back left corner.

Memorial to the firefighters who lost their lives in the Great Fire of 1910.

Shoshone Falls in full flow. It looked far different when Al Faussett went over on July 28, 1929.

AL FAUSSETT'S
$733-Ride

Just after noon on Sunday, July 28, 1929, spectators began gathering on the south bank of the Snake River a few miles east of Twin Falls. At five p.m., Al Faussett, a former lumberjack from Monroe, Washington, planned to do the impossible: ride a boat over Shoshone Falls.

During the previous three years, the lean daredevil had gone over six waterfalls in Washington and Oregon. Shoshone Falls, however, at 212 feet high, was to be his most formidable challenge. Faussett's 12-foot-long canoe resembled an outsized football, its wooden frame covered with orange canvas. Inside there was barely enough room to accommodate Faussett and the half-inflated inner tubes he intended using for padding.

Legionnaires sold tickets to those wanting to see the stunt up close: 50¢ for adults and 25¢ for children. Half the proceeds would go to the American Legion and the other half to Faussett. As the hot summer afternoon wore on, nearly 1,200 cars filled every flat space between the river and canyon rim. Idaho National Guardsmen, Twin Falls police, deputy sheriffs, and Boy Scouts helped with parking and crowd control. And it was fortunate they were there, for on three occasions the Boy Scouts, National Guardsmen, and a number of the spectators had to stomp out grassfires that threatened the autos.

The crowd eventually grew to 5,000 strong, which up to that time was the largest number of people ever assembled in south-central Idaho. A few of the more foolhardy spectators clambered atop the boulders sitting gray and dry in the riverbed. In 1929, like in summers today, most of the Snake's flow was diverted into irrigation canals at Milner Dam.

At 4:30 p.m. the Idaho Power Company opened Milner's floodgates, releasing a stream for Faussett to ride. Before climbing into his rift, the daredevil rechecked the galvanized wire that ran from a large rock in mid-river, through a three-inch eyebolt attached to the canoe's bow, and over the falls. Terry Prater sat in a motorboat at the bottom of the falls, holding the wire's free end. A large rocky knob protruded from the face of the falls, blocking Faussett's intended route. When the orange coracle plunged over the falls, Prater was to jerk the wire, maneuvering Faussett away from the lethal knob.

At 4:45 p.m. four detonations signaled the stunt would begin in 15 minutes. After stuffing one last inner tube inside the hull, Faussett pulled in his head, and an assistant sealed the canvas shut. Duncan Johnston and Jim Weaver pushed the boat into the river. Despite the gates of Milner Dam being wide open, the flow was barely deep enough for the craft to float.

Three more explosions marked there were but 10 minutes remaining. A cameraman in a motor launch at the base of the falls steadied himself while he focused his lens on the thin stream of water cascading into space. Nearby, Terry Prater stood up in his boat and pulled the slack from the wire he clutched in his gloved hands.

Two more blasts warned there were five minutes left. The crowd pressed forward, each person seeking the best vantage. Johnston and Weaver held Faussett's canoe in a small eddy, ready to shove it into the current.

At exactly 5 p.m. a single explosive clap brought down a curtain of silence as the crowd held its collective breath. After wishing Faussett "good luck," Johnston and Weaver pushed him into the current. As the football-shaped boat drifted toward the edge, Prater reeled in slack from the guidewire.

Above the falls Faussett's canvas hull scraped over a patch of rock. The boat stuck. Johnston and Weaver waded out to it and then muscled the craft into a deeper flow. Prater pulled the wire taut, directing Faussett toward the brink.

As the boat's orange bow edged over the falls, the cameraman turned his hand-crank, recording the momentous event for the newsreels. Terry Prater tightened his grip around the wire, waiting to deflect Faussett away from the protruding knob. The crowd dared not blink, lest it miss the plunge.

The canvas boat teetered at the precipitous drop, refusing

to go over. It had stuck on another rock. Once more Johnston and Weaver plodded through the shallows. Buttoned up inside as if he were a canned sardine, Faussett could do nothing but hope and pray.

After reaching the canoe, Johnston and Weaver strained against its stubborn weight, trying to move it without ripping the cloth hull. As the boat inched forward, the rock lip began to act like a fulcrum. Lifting the stern, Johnston and Weaver tilted the bow over the chasm.

And then it was gone. Prater yanked the wire, whipping Faussett away from the worrisome knob. The news photographer cranked the film through his camera, hoping he caught the bow as it shattered against a rock at the base of the falls. The spectators watched, too nervous to talk, fearing no one could live through such a terrible fall.

Two rescue boats towed Faussett to the south shore, where his orange cocoon was opened. Favoring his right hand, which he had broken, the plucky daredevil stepped out of his boat and waved. A moment later, a salvo of explosions announced Faussett was safe.

The American Legion sold $1,466 in tickets that day. For risking his life in a death-defying ride over Shoshone Falls, Al Faussett earned a whopping $733.

SIGHTS TO SEE

Shoshone Falls

From Blue Lakes Boulevard (US 93) in Twin Falls drive east three miles on Falls Avenue. Turn north (left) on E3300. In two miles descend to the overlook.

Shoshone Falls is most spectacular in the spring before the Snake River is diverted for irrigation. However, during the summer and early autumn, it more closely resembles what it looked like when Al Faussett took his daring ride.

"POTATOE?"

No Matter How It's Misspelled, An Idaho Spud is the World's Best

Mention "potato" and the typical American will think of a long, fat russet Burbank, its light brown skin pinched open and steaming, its starchy white pulp flaked apart and piled high with melting butter and dollops of fresh sour cream. Ask where the best potatoes are grown, and you'll most likely hear "Idaho."

Press your respondent about what other things he or she knows about potatoes, and you're apt to hear how nutritious they are and how they're loaded with good things like vitamin C and potassium, while being free from the bad stuff such as cholesterol and fat (if you don't count the butter and sour cream, that is). But hardly anyone will bring up the relationship between potatoes and presidential politics.

The most recent involvement occurred some years ago when Vice President Dan Quayle sank his Oval Office aspirations by adding the notorious ending "e" as he misspelled potato for a group of students.

His was a harmless blunder, hardly as serious as crying in public, which drowned Senator Edmund Muskie's presidential bid in 1972, or claiming to have been brainwashed by the Pentagon brass, which doomed George Romney during the Vietnam War. Still, Dan Quayle's gaffe made the evening news, and the rest, as they say, is history.

The potato is a tuber, not a root. Scientists describe a tuber as a stem that has evolved to live underground. The modern potato had its genesis about 7,000 years ago in the Andes Mountains of South America. Peruvians were the first to cultivate it, beginning around 200 BC. Spanish conquistadors introduced the potato to Europe in the 1500s, and during the next two centuries it spread across the entire continent.

The potato came to North America with the colonists in the 1600s and quickly took hold. Although Henry Spalding grew Idaho's first potatoes at his Lapwai Mission in 1837, the Gem State's prowess as a potato producer had to wait for a Massachusetts botanist and the Oregon Short Line Railroad.

In 1872 Luther Burbank developed a new breed of potato, which is now called the russet Burbank. Farmers in southeastern Idaho soon found that the area's rich volcanic soil and Burbank's tuber were as suited for each other as mashed potatoes and giblet gravy. However, it wasn't until the railroad arrived that Idaho farmers were able to introduce the rest of the nation to their superior spud.

Idaho now grows 10 billion pounds of potatoes each year. Although much of the crop ends up baked in traditional or microwave ovens, the lion's share is processed into french fries, which is how 50 percent of all potatoes are consumed.

No matter if Americans eat at McDonalds, Wendy's, or home, all of us love our french fries. Yet, if it hadn't been for presidential politics, the country may never have developed a taste for dipping a golden fried potato spear into a bowl of thick red catsup.

Francophile Thomas Jefferson, while he was President, served french fries to his White House guests. John Adams thought Jefferson was putting on airs with the imported novelty, but everyone else found the fries a delicious treat. French fries quickly caught on with the rest of the country, and, as they say, everything else is history.

Idaho Potato Museum

From I-15 Exit 93 drive into Blackfoot on the I-15 business loop for 1.2 miles and turn left on West Main Street. In 0.2 mile turn right into the parking lot beside the giant baked potato. Exposition address: 130 N.W. Main, Blackfoot, ID 83221.

Located in Bingham County, the heart of potato country, the museum celebrates Idaho's premier agricultural product. Displays tell the story of the potato's evolution from its origin in the Peruvian Andes to its refinement by the Luther Burbank.

Since the museum first opened in 1991, visitors from around the world have learned about one of mankind's most important crops. During your visit, don't fail to see the potato autographed by Vice President Quayle.

SUN VALLEY'S
Banana Boat Connection

Mention Sun Valley and most people will envision skiers schussing through untracked powder as they link turns down Bald Mountain. A few may also picture a robin's-egg-blue sky and a morning sun transposing the previous night's snowfall into a billion glistening diamonds. But few if any will think of banana boats.

Yet if it weren't for banana boats, Sun Valley's skiers would be hard-pressed to ascend "Mount Baldy's" 9,150 feet of elevation.

In 1935 when Averell Harriman began planning the nation's first destination ski resort, he had no thoughts of banana boats either. As chairman of the Union Pacific Railroad, he was concerned with adding passengers to his company's trains.

Competing railroads, such as the Santa Fe, Southern Pacific, and Canadian Pacific, could whisk their riders to the Grand Canyon, Palm Springs, or Lake Louise. The Union Pacific had no scenic wonders that could compare.

Having recently visited the Swiss Alps, Harriman had seen skiers flocking to resorts like St. Moritz. But in the United States, skiing was in its infancy.

About this time Harriman made the acquaintance of Count Felix Schaffgotsch, an Austrian who was working in New York City. In November 1935 the Count agreed to travel the western United States in order to find a fitting site for a ski resort. Naturally, Harriman insisted it be located in an area served by the Union Pacific.

Over the next two months Schaffgotsch eliminated one place after another: Mt. Rainier—too close to Seattle; Mt. Hood—too rainy; Yosemite National Park—too crowded. From Lake Tahoe to the San Bernardino Mountains and from Colorado to Utah, the likely locations faded into snowy disappointment.

The Ruud Mountain Chairlift: Sun Valley's banana boat connection.

Then in January 1936 the Count came to Idaho. Bill Hynes, the Union Pacific representative accompanying Schaffgotsch, showed him the country around Pocatello. The Count admitted there was plenty of snow, but the mountains didn't have the scenic backdrop he envisioned. He and Hynes headed over Teton Pass to Wyoming.

In Jackson Hole Schaffgotsch saw the peak of his dreams. The Grand Teton reminded him of the summits in his native Austria. Excitedly he wired Harriman he had found the spot; the snow and vistas were perfect. However, the State of Wyoming refused to open Teton Pass in the winter, and a southern approach was too far from a Union Pacific railhead. His mission a failure, the Count boarded a train for the East Coast, while Hynes headed to Boise.

The following day Hynes recounted the fruitless search to his friend, Joe Stemmer, director of Idaho's highways. Stemmer suggested the Count look at Ketchum. The Union Pacific owned a spur line to the old mining town, and Stemmer argued there had to be enough snow for skiing, since the railroad spent a fortune each winter keeping the tracks clear.

Hynes hurriedly dashed off a telegram, requesting Schaffgotsch meet him in Shoshone. When the wire caught up with the Count in Denver, he grabbed the next train for Idaho.

Because the winter rail service to Ketchum ran only three days per week, Hynes and Schaffgotsch drove from Shoshone, a gutsy decision since they made the trip in a blizzard. As they rode down Timmerman Hill into the Wood River Valley, their car slid into a snowbank, where it remained until a plow came by and pulled it out.

Upon finally reaching Ketchum, the two men took lodgings in a small, run-down motor court. Unaccustomed to having an urbane guest like Schaffgotsch, the proprietor handed him a shovel so he could clear a path to his cabin.

The next morning the Count and Hynes awakened to a blue, sun-filled sky. After breakfast, Schaffgotsch put on a pair of skis, which he had brought with him, and climbed atop Dollar Mountain. The view was stunning, and when he skied down, the powdery snow billowed around his head. Two days later the Count telegraphed Harriman that he had found the ideal setting for the resort.

The Union Pacific chairman arrived in February via his private rail car. Agreeing with the Count that the valley was perfect, Harriman paid $39,000 for the 4,300-acre sheep ranch of Ernest Brass, which was about a mile outside of Ketchum.

In March Harriman enlisted Charlie Proctor and John E. P. Morgan, two prominent American skiers, to position the resort's ski runs amid the nearby hills. Meantime Count Schaffgotsch wandered the ranch with a deck chair as he sought the best views and best sun. After sitting in countless locations, he pointed at a patch of snow-covered ground and announced the lodge should be built there, in the middle of a hayfield.

While Schaffgotsch, Proctor, and Morgan were scouting the ranch, Harriman hired Steve Hannagan, the eastern publicist who had transformed a worthless stretch of Florida sand into Miami Beach. One of Hannagan's first recommendations was to name the new resort Sun Valley. Unable to imagine why anyone except a crazy person would choose to vacation in the snow, Hannagan insisted the resort have certain frills that would make the cold "bearable."

As the resort's plans rapidly expanded to include a heated swimming pool, ice rink, and bowling alley, the budget ballooned. By the time construction crews poured the concrete for the foundation, the lodge had grown from a $500,000, 120-room hotel to one with 220 rooms, costing $1.5 million. Then as the hotel began to take shape, the architect discovered the building envelope extended beyond the Brass Ranch. Fortunately for Averell Harriman, the Ketchum Livestock Association, which owned the infringed land, agreed to sell the Union Pacific another 40 acres.

With the hotel construction underway, Steve Hannagan turned his attention to the ski runs, insisting they be equipped with "mechanical devices" to move the skiers uphill. That someone would actually climb a mountain just to ski down was beyond his comprehension.

European resorts transported their skiers via aerial tramways. In the eastern United States, a few ski areas had the newfangled rope tows and J-bars, whereas Yosemite used an Upski, a six-person toboggan that was winched up while being counterbalanced by an empty, descending toboggan.

Hannagan's suggestion for mechanical ascenders was assigned to the Union Pacific's engineers in Omaha, Nebraska. Two hoists were required, since Charlie Proctor and John Morgan had decided that both Proctor and Dollar Mountains should have ski runs.

While several of the engineers began adapting the J-bar and rope tow to Sun Valley's slopes, others examined the feasibility of cog railways. Among the engineers was Jim Curran, who had recently worked for Paxton-Vierling Ironworks, where he designed conveyor hooks that loaded bananas aboard a ship in a continuous flow instead of one bunch at a time.

As Curran thought about moving Sun Valley's skiers, he couldn't get the banana conveyor out of his mind. If he could substitute chairs for the hooks, he knew he'd be able to carry more skiers than either an Upski or tram. As an added benefit, chairs would deliver skiers atop a mountain without the burning thigh muscles which were by-products of the rope tow and J-bar.

After making a blueprint of his idea, Curran showed it to his boss, who felt it was too dangerous. Soon afterwards Charlie Proctor visited Omaha to check on the engineers' progress. As he flipped through drawings of cog railways and rope tows, he saw Curran's design for the mobile chair and asked the young engineer how it worked.

Intrigued by the concept, Proctor recommended Curran's chair to Averell Harriman, who then asked the engineers to build a prototype. The assignment was given to Jim Curran.

Since no one knew how fast a skier could be safely picked up, Curran fashioned a wooden scaffold on the bed of a Ford utility truck and suspended a chair from its side. Wearing a pair of skis, John Morgan, who had come from Idaho to help, stood on straw as a driver slowly edged the truck and chair toward him. When the skis refused to slide properly, Morgan switched to roller skates.

Beginning at four feet per minute, Curran increased the truck's speed until the chair was snatching Morgan at a brisk 7½ feet per second.

On August 26 Curran began constructing his skier conveyors, which he called monocables, on Dollar and Proctor Mountains. Since the word chairlift wasn't in the dictionary, the publicist Steve Hannagan advertised the devices as "chair-type lifts."

In early November the first chairlift was ready to test. Twenty female volunteers stepped up to the Proctor Lift, letting its chairs gently pluck them off the ground. Some of the ladies waved to the crowd of onlookers, while others gripped the bars attaching the chairs to the moving cable until their knuckles blanched. Suddenly the lift motor stalled, leaving the women suspended like so many bunches of bananas.

While Curran frantically searched for the cause of the stoppage, workmen lowered the nervous volunteers with ropes. After replacing a blown fuse, Curran called for the ladies to try again. When none came forward, the resort manager ordered his secretary, Florence Law, onto the lift. This time everything worked perfectly, making Ms. Law the world's first official chairlift passenger.

On December 21, 1936, the Sun Valley Resort opened on schedule. Guests included Hollywood producer David O. Selznick and his wife, actresses Joan Bennett and Claudette Colbert, and a host of America's other rich and famous.

The resort lavished its patrons with the finest food and wine, entertained them with a live orchestra, let them swim in a heated, outdoor pool and skate on man-made ice. Sun Valley offered its guests every amenity . . . except snow. It was early January before skiers could use Jim Curran's chairlifts for anything other than a scenic ride.

SIGHTS TO SEE

Sun Valley Lodge and Inn

Located in the Sun Valley Village one mile NE of Ketchum on Sun Valley Road.

Bald Mountain (or as the locals call it, "Mount Baldy")

Access the mountain from either River Run Plaza in south Ketchum or Warm Springs Lodge in west Ketchum.

Dollar Mountain

Access the mountain from Elkhorn Road in Sun Valley. "Dollar's" lifts and easier runs allow beginning skiers to hone their skills before tackling "Baldy."

Although the 1936 chairlifts no longer exist, at the end of Fairway Road in Sun Valley you can see the Ruud Mountain Lift, which was built from Jim Curran's original design.

River Run Lodge at Sun Valley.

BIBLIOGRAPHY

"Agaidüka, Ancient Fishermen of Southern Idaho." *Cultural Resource Information Series*, Number 2. Bureau of Land Management.

Alt, David D. and Donald W. Hyndman. *Roadside Geology of Idaho*. MT: Mountain Press Publishing Co., 1989.

Ambrose, Stephen E. *Undaunted Courage: Meriwether Lewis, Thomas Jefferson, and the Opening of the American West*. NY: Simon & Schuster, 1996.

Andersen, Shea. "Chairlift Originated in Sun Valley." *Sun Valley Guide*, Winter 1996-97, p. 49.

Andersen, Shea. "Sun Valley: From Harriman to Holding." *Sun Valley Guide*, Winter 1996-97, p. 42-5.

"Another Pioneer Gone Beyond, Heart Trouble Takes 'Rube' Robbins, Trusted Public Servant for Many Years." *Idaho Daily Statesman*, May 2, 1908, p. 5.

"Answers about the Aquifer." Brochure from the Idaho National Engineering Laboratory. Department of Energy.

Arnold, R. Ross. *Indian Wars of Idaho*. ID: The Caxton Printers, Ltd., 1932.

Arrington, Leonard J. *History of Idaho*, Volumes 1 and 2. ID: University of Idaho Press, 1994.

"A Woman Perishes in Snow." *Elmore Bulletin* [Mountain Home, Idaho], May 27, 1896, p. 3.

"Baker Caves." *Cultural Resource Information Series*, Number 1. Bureau of Land Management.

Bluestein, Sheldon. *Exploring Idaho's High Desert*, Second Edition. ID: Challenge Expedition Co., 1991.

Campbell, Mrs. Paul. "Benoni Morgan Hudspeth." *Idaho Yesterdays*, Volume 12, Number 3, Fall 1986, p. 9-13.

Carlson, Dave. "Stark Realities, Craters of the Moon," *Idaho Motorist*, Summer 1995, p. 8-10.

Chittenden, Hiram Martin. *The American Fur Trade of the Far West*, Volumes 1 and 2, 1986 Bison Book Edition. NE: University of Nebraska Press, 1935.

"City of Rocks, Official Map and Guide." National Park Service, 1994.

Coleman, Louis C. and Leo Rieman. *Captain John Mullan; His Life Building the Mullan Road*. Montreal, Canada: Payette Radio Ltd., 1968.

Conley, Cort. *Idaho for the Curious, a Guide*, First Edition. ID: Backeddy Books, 1982.

Cordes, Jeff. "Sun Valley Lodge Born, The Nine Months of '36." *Idaho Mountain Express*, December 23, 1981, p. C1-7.

"Craters of the Moon Guide." National Park Service, Summer 1995.

"Craters of the Moon, Official Map and Guide." National Park Service, 1995.

"Dare-Devil's Leap at Shoshone Falls Kindles Interest." *Twin Falls Daily News*, July 28, 1929, p. 8.

d'Easum, Dick. "A Bit of a Chill at Atlanta." *Idaho Sunday Statesman*, October 23, 1960, Section One, p. 4.

DeVoto, Bernard. *Across the Wide Missouri*. MA: Houghton Mifflin Co., 1947.

DeVoto, Bernard. *The Course of Empire*. MA: Houghton Mifflin Co., 1952.

DeVoto, Bernard, ed. *The Journals of Lewis and Clark*. MA: Houghton Mifflin Co., 1953.

DeVoto, Bernard. *The Year of Decision, 1846*. MA: Houghton Mifflin Co., 1942.

Dockery, Eva Hunt, ed. "Rube Robbins, Pioneer Marshal, Scout, Indian Fighter—Man Who Never Knew Fear." *Idaho Sunday Statesman*, August 24, 1913, Second Section, p. 3.

Dockery, Eva Hunt, ed. "Rube Robbins and the Silver Creek Duel." *Idaho Sunday Statesman*, August 31, 1913, Second Section, p. 12.

Dockery, Eva Hunt, ed. "Monument to be Erected Soon to the Memory of Rube Robbins." *Idaho Sunday Statesman*, May 10, 1914, Second Section, p. 10.

"East Goes West to Idaho's Sun Valley, Society's Newest Winter Playground." *Life Magazine*, March 8, 1937, p. 20-7.

"Faussett Conquers Shoshone Falls in 'Football' Canoe." *Twin Falls Daily News*, July 30, 1929, p. 8.

Fehrenbacher, Don E. *The Era of Expansion, 1800-1848*. NY: John Wiley & Sons, Inc., 1969.

"Fort Hall, 1834-1856." *Idaho Historical Series*, Number 17, August 1968.

Frazer, Robert W. *Forts of the West*. OK: University of Oklahoma Press, 1965.

Germain, Jeanette. "Folklore Partly True, Sun Valley Boasts First Chair Lift in World." *Idaho Mountain Express*, December 23, 1981, p. C8-10.

Gray, Shawn. "The Early Years of Sun Valley Resort: Depression, War, Reconstruction, 1936-1950." Private Research Report, May 31, 1985. Courtesy of the Regional History Department of the Community Library, Ketchum, Idaho.

Great Rift, Proposed Wilderness Final Environmental Impact Statement. DC: Bureau of Land Management, 1980.

Grover, David H. *Diamondfield Jack, A Study in Frontier Justice*, 1986 Edition. OK: University of Oklahoma Press, 1968.

Hackett, Dr. Bill, Dr. Jack Pelton, and Dr. Chyuck Brockway. *Geohydrologic Story of the Eastern Snake River Plane and the Idaho National Engineering Laboratory*. DC: Department of Energy, 1986.

Hart, Arthur A. "Famed Indian Fighter Once Kept Boise Peace." *Idaho Statesman*, June 22, 1970, p. 10.

Hart, Arthur A. "Temperance Movement Enlisted Famous Marshal." *Idaho Statesman*, July 9, 1973, p. 8.

Hart, Arthur A. "They Went That-a-Way." *Idaho Statesman*, December 22, 1975, p. 10B.

Hutchinson, Daniel J. and Larry R. Jones, eds. *Emigrant Trails of Southern Idaho*, Idaho Cultural Resource Series, Number 1. ID: Idaho State Historical Society and Bureau of Land Management, 1993.

"Idaho's Hagerman Valley." Information Sheet, Idaho Travel Council, 1995.

Information Please Almanac, 48th Edition. MA: Houghton Mifflin Co., 1995.

Johnson, Lamont. "The Saga of Peg-Leg Annie." *Seeing Idaho*, November 1937, p. 18-19.

Josephy, Alvin M., Jr. *The Indian Heritage of American*, 1991 Revised Edition. MA: Houghton Mifflin Co., 1968.

Key, Francis Scott. "The Star-Spangled Banner." America's National Anthem.

Kjelstrom, L.C. "Assessment of Spring Discharge to the Snake River, Milner Dam to King Hill, Idaho." *Water Fact Sheet* of the US Geological Survey, Open-File Report, p. 92-147, 1992.

"Lava Hot Springs." *Southeastern Idaho Tourist Guide*, 1996, p. 58-66.

Lavender, David. *Fort Laramie and the Changing Frontier*, National Park Handbook 118. DC: National Park Service Division of Publications, 1983.

Lecture about Camas by a National Park Ranger at the Spalding Site of the Nez Perce National Historical Park, July 1995.

"Lewis and Clark Trail." Map and Brochure, National Park Service, 1991.

Lindsley, Margaret Hawkes. *Andrew Henry, Mine and Mountain Major*. WY: Jelm Mountain Publications, 1990.

Lopez, Tom. *Exploring Idaho's Mountains*. WA: The Mountaineers, 1990.

Lovell, Edith Haroldsen. *Benjamin Bonneville, Soldier of the American Frontier*. UT: Horizon Publishers & Distributors, Inc., 1992.

Madsen, Brigham D. *Chief Pocatello, The "White Plume."* UT: University of Utah Press, 1986.

"Massacre Rocks Historical Leaflet." Friends of Massacre Rocks.

"Massacre Rocks State Park, Yahandeka Self-Guiding Nature Trail." Guide from Friends of Massacre Rocks.

McPhee, John. *Basin and Range*, 1990 Edition. NY: Noonday Press, 1980.

"Monument at Rube Robbins' Grave To Be Dedicated Decoration Day." *Idaho Sunday Statesman*, May 17, 1914, Second Section, p. 2.

Morgan, Dale L. *Jedediah Smith and the Opening of the West*, 1964 Bison Book Edition. NE: University of Nebraska Press, 1953.

Newman, Peter Charles. *Caesars of the Wilderness, Company of Adventurers*, Volume II. NY: Penguin Books, 1987.

O'Connor, Jim E. *Hydrology, Hydraulics, and Geomorphology of the Bonneville Flood*, Special Paper 274. CO: The Geological Society of America, Inc., 1993.

Official Idaho State Travel Guide. Idaho Division of Tourism Development, 1995.

Ognibene, Peter J. "At the First Ski Spa, Stars Outshone the Sun and Snow." *Smithsonian*, December 1984, p. 109-19.

Oppenheimer, Doug and Jim Poore. *Sun Valley, A Biography*. ID: Beatty Books, 1976.

Oral Interview with Hilda Goddard of Mackay, Idaho, on January 18, 1996.

Oral Interview with Jack Sibbach, Director of Marketing and Public Relations of the Sun Valley Resort, Sun Valley, Idaho, on December 27, 1996.

Oral Interview with Wiley Smith of Mackay, Idaho, on January 18, 1996.

Parfit, Michael. "The Floods that Carved the West." *Smithsonian*, Volume 26, Number 1. April 1995, p. 48-59.

Pawbitse. Interpreted by Herman War Jack. Written by Byrd Trego. "Our Last War with the Paleface." *Idaho Republican* [Blackfoot, Idaho], June 16, 1932, p. 2.

Penson, Betty. "As She Says, Nostalgic Readers Write Footnotes to Local Tales." Letters by Hazel Schooler Rhoades and Maysie Heron, *Idaho Statesman*, July 13, 1975, p. 12C.

Perkins, Barbara, ed. "Sun Valley Lodge Turns 60." *Idaho Mountain Express*, December 18, 1996, p. B1 and B3.

Robinson, Russell. *The Story of the Shoshone Indian Ice Caves*. ID: Ice Cave Co., Inc., 1989.

Rozwenc, Edwin C. *The Making of American Society*, Volume I to 1877. MA: Allyn and Bacon, Inc., 1972.

Schwantes, Carlos A. *In Mountain Shadows, A History of Idaho*. NE: University of Nebraska Press, 1991.

Shallat, Todd, ed. *Snake, The Plain and Its People*. ID: Boise State University, 1994.

Smith, Michele McIntyre. "Peg Leg Annie McIntyre." Historical Note, Idaho State Historical Society, April 19, 1991.

"Snake River Canyon." Information Sheet, Idaho Travel Council, 1995.

Space, Ralph S. *The Lolo Trail*. ID: Printcraft Printing, 1970.

Spellenberg, Richard. *The Audubon Society Field Guide to North American Wildflowers*, Western Region. NY: Alfred A. Knopf, 1979.

Stanton, Clark T. "Idaho Indian War of 1878." *North Side News* [Jerome, Idaho], April 27, 1933, p. 1.

"Sun Valley Winter, 1996-97 Season." Information Brochure of the Sun Valley Resort.

Swanson, Earl H. "The Snake River Plain." *Idaho Historical Series*, Number 11, December 1974, p. 1-12.

Taylor, Dorice. *Sun Valley*. ID: Ex Libris, 1980.

"The Snake River Plain Aquifer." Information Pamphlet of the Idaho Water Resources Research Institute, University of Idaho.

Unruh, John D., Jr. *The Plains Across*, 1982 Illini Books Edition. IL: University of Illinois Press, 1979.

Utley, Robert M. and Wilcomb E. Washburn. *Indian Wars*, 1987 Edition. MA: Houghton Mifflin Co., 1977.

"Views from the Visitor Center." Information Sheet, Idaho Travel Council, 1994.

Walker, Eugene H. "A Geologic History of the Snake River Country of Idaho." *Idaho Historical Series*, Number 8, September 1963, p. 1-15.

Welch, Julia Conway. *Gold Town to Ghost Town, The Story of Silver City, Idaho*. ID: University of Idaho Press, 1982.

Whitehead, R.L. "Geohydrologic Framework of the Snake River Plain Regional Aquifer System, Idaho and Eastern Oregon." *US Geological Survey Professional Paper 1408-B*, 1992.

Whitehead, R.L. *Ground Water Atlas of the United States*, Segment 7. VA: US Geological Survey, 1994.

Wyeth, Nathaniel. Wyeth's "stone" quotation taken from a display at the Fort Hall replica in Pocatello, Idaho.

Other Books by R. G. Robertson

Rotting Face: Smallpox and the American Indian
Caxton Press
ISBN 0-87004-419-2

Competitive Struggle: America's Western Fur Trading Posts, 1764-1865
Caxton Press
ISBN 978-0-87004-510-3

Idaho Echoes in Time *(Out of Print)*
Tamarack Books
ISBN 1-886609-12-8

Beyond the Yellowstone
CreateSpace Independent Publishing
ISBN 978-1499215755

The Jewel of Fort Union

Land of the Crow

Return to the Hell Gate

Fur Trade Trilogy

Silver City Justice

Daughters of the King

R. G. Robertson served as a U.S. Marine Corps officer in the Vietnam War from the start of the infamous Tet Offensive in late January 1968 until February 1969. After completing his military service, he earned an MBA from the University of Michigan. During nineteen years in the investment business, he was a partner at Hambrecht & Quist and later a self-employed options market maker on the Pacific Stock Exchange in San Francisco.

In 1990 he and his wife, Karen, moved from the Bay Area to Sun Valley, Idaho, where he began writing not only about Idaho's history and geology but also about mountain men and the fur trade. In researching his books, the couple drove thousands of miles across the western United States, visiting the sites where *Idaho Inside and Out* and R. G.'s other books take place. In 1999 they relocated to Scottsdale, Arizona, and in 2014 they moved back to Idaho, where they live today.

In addition to writing, R. G. enjoys mountain climbing, hiking, skiing, biking, watching movies, and traveling the American West.

Karen Robertson is a native of Oregon. After receiving BS degrees in history and political science from Portland State University, she worked in the investment business in Oregon and California. Karen's interest in photography began in the 1950s and early 1960s when she and her family modeled for their personal friend, Ray Atkeson, Photographer Laureate of Oregon. Karen now devotes her time to photography, traveling, skiing, biking, and climbing mountains. Her photographs have been published in R.G.'s nonfiction books and in his magazine and newspaper articles.

CPSIA information can be obtained
at www.ICGtesting.com
Printed in the USA
JSHW022042040621
15583JS00004B/5

9 780870 046377